Y0-CXM-128

THE MANY SPEECHES OF CHIEF

SEATTLE (SEATHL):

THE MANIPULATION OF THE
RECORD

ON BEHALF OF

RELIGIOUS, POLITICAL AND

ENVIRONMENTAL CAUSES

ELI GIFFORD

Other books by Eli Gifford

How Can One Sell the Air?: Chief Seattle's Vision   1992
                                                       reprint 2005

Copyright 2015 by Eli Gifford

CreateSpace Independent Publishing Platform
North Charleston, SC

William Arrowsmith's adaptation of Chief Seathl's speech is included
with permission from his estate.
Ted Perry's script for the movie HOME is included with Mr. Perry's
permission.
John Stevens' adaptation of Perry' script is included with the
Southern Baptists Radio and Television Commission's permission.
Adaptation of Perry's script by Northwest Airlines magazine *Passages*
is included with Northwest Airlines permission

Library of Congress Cataloguing in Publication Data

Gifford, Eli, 1951-
        The Many Speeches of Chief Seattle (Seathl): The
        Manipulation of the Record on Behalf of Religious, Political
        and Environmental Causes
                p.   cm.
        Includes bibliographical references.
        Contents: Chief Seattle's speeches as recorded by Dr.
        Henry Smith (1854, published in 1887)—Historical
        information and background— Adaptation by Frederic
        Grant-- Adaptation Clarence B. Bagley--Adaptation John M.
        Rich--Adaptation by Roberta Frye Watt--[Speech] by Ted
        Perry inspired by Chief Seattle—Adaptation by William
        Arrowsmith—Adaptation by John Stevens and Southern
        Baptists Radio and Television Commission—Adaptation by
        Northwest Airlines magazine Passages—

        LCCN 2015917885
        ISBN 10: 151-87494-96
        ISBN 13: 978-1-51874-949-0

        1. Seattle, Chief, 1790-1866—Oratory. 2. Speeches,
        addresses, etc., Suquamish. 3. Suquamish Indians—Land
        Tenure. 4. Human Ecology. I. Title

ALL RIGHTS RESERVED. No part of this book may be reproduced in any form or by any means, electronic or mechanical, including photocopying, recording or by any information retrieval system without written permission of the publisher.

To Barbara Chapman, my wife, for her relentless red pen in editing.

To Ted Perry, Professor of Film and Media Culture, who has spent nearly four decades trying to set the record straight.

To Edward Castillo, Professor of Native American Studies, whose confidence and unwavering support in seeing this published has been pivotal

To Dan Markwyn, Professor of United States History, who chaired my thesis committee demanding excellence from me.

And to all the previous researchers whose work made this book possible

TABLE OF CONTENTS

FOREWORD

Eli Gifford provides a very clear context to the person of Chief Seattle (Seathl), and how his historical role and his speeches have been manipulated for their own agenda by religious, political and environmental causes. While my own personal role in this history is minor, it seems larger because of the public's needy response to a text that I fabricated, and which came to have a life of its own. To some small extent the only thing that is missing from Eli's account is how often the text has been used – chorales, Australian folk songs, oratorios, often quoted in books, articles graduate theses, even bumper stickers. I still get requests for its use and even translation, and I always say yes if the credit says that I wrote the text and that its inspiration was a speech that Seattle supposedly gave. I say "supposedly" because I have questions, as do others, of the accuracy of a text published by a white man of what he heard thirty-three years earlier. Reading Eli's account, I am more convinced than ever that Dr. Henry Smith's version was a fabrication.

The great mystery to me was why so many people responded to what I wrote. Eli says when he first read my text, it fit his worldview at the time. No doubt that is what the speech's message meant to some others. We always pounce on evidence that supports our worldview. We also like legends and myths, of course; they provide a simple spin on the chaos and complexity of life. Knowing nothing else about Chief Seattle, we read the text and see a Native American like Chief Seattle as the image of the noble savage. It's not who he truly is but what he stands for– a simple existence where one lives in harmony with the physical world. Wrong. On our haughty pedestal, we acknowledge the Native Americans' connection to the natural and animal kingdoms – it fits our worldview - but we forget we also belong to the same kingdoms. What a shame that we ignore our heritage; it limits our identity.

I first heard a version of the text read by William Arrowsmith at the first Environmental Day celebration in 1970. I was there and heard him. He was a close friend. Arrowsmith's version hinted at how difficult it was for Seattle to understand the white man's attitude toward land, water, air, and animals. For the soundtrack for a documentary I had already proposed about the environment, I decided to write a new version, elaborating on and heightening what was hinted at in Arrowsmith's text.

Eli provides accurately the rest of the history of my involvement and he details my mistakes. Some of my statements only apply to the Plains Indians and their environment, not those in the Northwest. While it would be easy to hide behind the producer's decision, without my permission, to delete my "Written by" credit when the film was finished and aired on television, the real problem is that I should not have used the name of an actual human being, Chief Seattle. That I could put words into the mouth of someone I did not know, particularly a Native American, is pure hubris if not racist. While there has been some progress in our knowledge of Native Americans, we really know very little. What we think we know is mediated by films, chance encounters, words, images and other stereotypes. They serve our worldview but they are not true.

That I am extremely indebted to the work of Eli is a great understatement, but I am certainly not the only reader who will be very grateful.

Ted Perry Professor of Film and Media Culture

September 2015

PREFACE

Sitting in a JC history class in 1985, the professor read the environmental version of Chief Seathl's speech. I was deeply moved and dumbfounded. How could a Native American in 1854 give a speech that was so accurate in its prophecies envisioning what the Euro-Americans were going to do to the land and the consequences of those actions? Seathl didn't. A professor in 1971 wrote that speech.

The purpose of this book is to document the origins of the various speeches attributed to Chief Seathl and to identify the reasons the speech was manipulated. To document the evolution and the manipulation of Seathl's speech, a number of sources were used: newspapers, oral histories, autobiographies, biographies, personal interviews and letters from the people involved in the manipulation of Seathl's words.

Chief Seathl did give a speech to Governor Stevens, but we cannot be certain if the original transcription is Seathl's words. Dr. Henry A. Smith wrote the original version of the speech from notes he claimed to have taken while Seathl spoke. The authenticity of the sentiment expressed in the original version is also debatable. However, in the foreword of the 2005 revised edition of *How Can One Sell the Air?: Chief's Seattle's Vision*, Marilyn Jones writes, "in 1982 after reviewing the notes from Dr. Henry Smith's personal journals the Suquamish Tribe placed the stamp approval on his version of the speech."[1] The environmental version attributed to Chief Seathl was written in 1971.

The first four chapters of the book focus on the original version of the speech. In first chapter, I give a brief account of Seathl's life. In the second chapter, I sketch the lives of Smith and Stevens, why they crossed paths and the exact date the speech was spoken. The third

---

[1] Eli Gifford and R. Michael Cook, eds. *How Can One Sell the Air*, 6. Hereinafter cited in text as Gifford, *How Can One Sell the Air*.

chapter is an attempt to answer the question: Why the thirty-three year lapse between the time Seathl spoke and when Smith published the speech? The fourth chapter is a comparison of Smith's version and the only other recorded speeches by Seathl: two recorded by government interpreters and the other by someone who spoke Chinook jargon fluently. I compare the three speeches with Smith's noting the differences in the use of metaphors and similes and the similarity of style of the three speeches when compared to Smith's version. The fifth chapter deals with Bagley's and Rich's alterations of the speech and who may have been the first to unearth Smith's original version. The information in all of these five chapters is gleaned from a mixture of diaries, memoirs, newspaper accounts, the research done by others and in the case of Seathl, interviews given by his contemporaries.

The last two chapters focus on the environmental versions of the speech. At the time I began the research, all of the people who were involved with the environmental speech in one way or the other were still alive, so much my information is based on letters and telephone interviews. Professor William Arrowsmith died a number of years ago, and John Stevens, the producer who added the religiosity to the environmental speech, died a few years ago. Only Professor Ted Perry, who wrote the original environmental version, is alive. I am also indebted to those who have published their own research on the environmental speech.

My intention in writing this is to compile the history of the many speeches attributed to Chief Seathl and to try to shed some light as to why so many people altered his speech to meet their own agenda. I also wanted to gather all the research done by others, establish the fact the speech was spoken, and give an accurate account of the history of the environmental speech. No one has attempted to bring all these variations of the speech together, and this is the only account that all three men responsible for the environmental version agree is an accurate account of what happened.

Chief Seathl did give a speech on January 12, 1854. At the present time there is no text that can be identified positively as the words of Seathl. The environmental version of the speech was written in 1970 by Ted Perry, who at the time was an associate professor of Theatre Arts at the University of Texas at Austin. Originally, Perry wrote it as a film script for the Baptist Radio and Television Commission. It was subsequently edited by John Stevens, a producer working for the Baptist Radio and Television Commission.

All the environmental versions are based on the film script that Stevens edited.

Introduction

I first heard Chief Seathl's famous environmental speech (or letter, depending on your source), in 1983 in a college history class. As the professor read the speech I was deeply moved by the pain of Chief Seathl's words, his thoughts and his visions. In that short speech, (the professor's source identified it as a letter sent to President Franklin Pierce), Seathl said everything I wanted a Native American to say.[2] It fit perfectly with my worldview at the time. I had identified Western culture as the cause of the ills in the world and the Native American culture as the remedy for those ills. What could be more fitting than having the prophecies of a Native American spoken 129 years ago fulfilled in our time? Americans were beginning to comprehend the gravity of mistreating the environment. The speech wrapped my romanticism of the Native Americans neatly in a package. I conveniently ignored the historical impossibilities. In the late eighties, I read it to my high school history classes with all the depth of emotion I felt. It was not until 1990 that I took my first serious look at the speech.

In a class on the study of language, I decided to learn Plains Indian Sign language and sign Seathl's "environmental" speech. While I was practicing, I came across a book titled *North American Indian Reader* and it had the first speech attributed to Seathl, not the environmental one. The two speeches had nothing in common. The original speech had no environmental messages, no forgiveness of the white brother, no God who was understanding and loving; worst of all no prophecies.

---

[2] Over the years there has been considerable confusion as to whether this environmental version was a speech given by Seathl to Governor Stevens or a letter written by Seathl to President Franklin Pierce.

My first reaction was how dare they print such an inaccurate speech and my second was, either one or both of these are wrong.

I mentioned this to the Chair of the Native American Studies at Sonoma State University, Edward Castillo, and he spoke of his doubts as to the authenticity of the environmental speech. Historically, Chief Seathl could not have seen a "smoking iron horse" or the slaughter of buffalo in 1854. The only possibility would have been if Seathl had seen this in a vision. Professor Castillo suggested I research the origins of these two speeches; and so began my seven-year odyssey. He provided me with the encouragement to research and complete this book. His confidence and unwavering support in seeing this published has been pivotal

What started out as a paper I presented in 1993 has become a master's thesis, a short book on speech's origin and environmental version and now this book. Twenty-three years ago, I never intended to dig as deeply as I have to unravel the story, but my committee chairperson Professor Daniel Markwyn was a relentless taskmaster. I am forever grateful to him. Even though I would sit in his office and argue and walk out grumbling, this book is a reflection of his high standards.

When I first tried to reconcile the two versions of the speech, I hit a number of dead ends. But once I located Professor Rudolph Kaiser's essay on his research of the speech and contacted research librarian Rick Caldwell at the Seattle Museum of History and Industry, the pieces slowly started to fall into place. Kaiser was the first person to connect Professor William Arrowsmith to the environmental version. I am indebted to Rick Caldwell for his generosity in sharing his own research and that of other scholars associated with the museum. Whatever request I had, for information, for photocopies, for names of other researchers, Rick provided. He continually helped me with my research throughout the years.

I was fortunate to speak with Professor William Arrowsmith a number of times before he died. He was able to fill gaps of information to which only he was privy. He never begrudged his time to help me sort out the various missing puzzles of "Chief Seattle's Environmental Speech." Both he and Professor Perry readily answered my questions even though they had repeated the same answers over the last thirty-five years. They have done all they could to dispel the myth of the environmental version and were willing to repeat the answers one more time for me.

Professor Perry has been an invaluable help in researching this book. We have spoken over the phone many times and corresponded through letters and emails as he continually attempts to set the record straight. I am grateful for the time he took to read this book and the suggestions he gave me.

I would be remiss not to include Puget Sound reporter Janice Krenmayr, who was probably the first to notice that the environmental version published in the 1970s was not the original version published in 1887. She was the first to research and publish her findings in a local newspaper. She was able to connect Professor Arrowsmith to the environmental version and interview him, but there the trail ended. It would be left to Professor Kaiser to connect Professor Perry to the environmental version.

As the story began to unfold a number of questions remained unanswered. For example, I continued to puzzle over the thirty-three year delay between the time Chief Seathl gave his speech and publication of the speech. Dr. Henry A. Smith claimed he took notes as Seathl spoke. Why did he wait so long to publish the transcription of his notes? I initially assumed that Smith felt a need to defend the Pacific Northwest tribes since the speech presented them in such a favorable light; except there was no need to defend these tribes or any other Native American tribe in 1887. Rick Caldwell of the Seattle Museum of History and Industry advised me to contact David Buerge, a writer living in the Puget Sound, who had been studying Seathl and Smith for years. Buerge believed Smith wrote the article in response to the city politics of Seattle. Smith used Seathl and the plight of his people in 1854 as a metaphor to explain what was happening to Smith's fellow pioneers in 1887. The more research I did the more obvious it became that Buerge might have found the reason Smith waited thirty-three years to publish the speech. All of the references to Buerge that I use are from articles he wrote in the local Puget Sound newspapers. He continues to write articles documenting what he has found and is about to publish his long awaited book. I'm indebted for the help he has given me.

We may never know what Seathl said to Governor Isaac I. Stevens that fateful January day in 1854. We know Seathl did not speak in the Victorian style of Smith's original version. But what of the thoughts, the beliefs, the deep sadness and despair for his peoples' plight, the feeling that fate offered his people nothing but the darkness of night that is found in Smith's version? We can only speculate as to its veracity. When I spoke with Marilyn Jones of the Suquamish Nation, she said according to their traditions Dr. Smith consulted the tribal elders numerous times before publishing the speech in the local paper in 1887. She also said the elders saw the notes Dr. Smith took while he listened to Seathl speak to Governor Stevens.[3] David Buerge believes that underlying the Victorian verbiage of Smith's version lies the essential message Seathl was trying to communicate. I remain unconvinced.

On the other hand, we do know the origins of the environmental speech. Professor Ted Perry, who wrote the first environmental version, and the producer, John Stevens, who edited Perry's version adding the religiosity and other phrases, for the most part agree as to what happened. Despite the fact these are not the words of Chief Seathl, it is of utmost importance to validate the message and the words found in the environmental version. They are true whether spoken by a Native American 161 years ago or written by a playwright forty-five years ago. The problem is our need to surround the speech with mystique and prophecy to legitimize the message. As Rick Caldwell said, "It doesn't sound the same if it was produced by a guy named Ted."[4]

Seathl's speech has been altered many times in the last 128 years, but five stages of the speech's transformation can be identified. The first was Dr. Smith's Victorian translation that he published in 1887. Forty years later two Puget Sound men ushered in the second stage by altering Smith's version, omitting some of Smith's sentences, editing others and adding their own words and sentences. Clarence Bagley was the first of the two to publish his version in his book on the local history. A few years later, John Rich privately published a booklet that included his alterations to Smith's version.

The third transformation marked the beginning of a significant chapter in the speech. In the late sixties a professor at the University of Texas, William Arrowsmith, came across the speech and attempted to translate Smith's original version removing the Victorian verbiage and following closer to what Seathl might have said.

---

[3] Marilyn Jones interview by author, 14 September 2007, Sebastopol, California, telephone. Hereafter cited in the text as Jones, 14 September 2007.

[4] Stephen Strauss, "Mind and Matter," *The Globe and Mail*, 8 February 1992, D8. Hereafter cited in the text as Strauss, "Mind of Matter."

The fourth stage was in 1970 when a friend of Arrowsmith and an assistant professor at the University of Texas, Ted Perry, wrote a film script based on Arrowsmith's translation. Perry had been commissioned by the Southern Baptists Radio and Television Commission to write three film scripts of his choice. His purpose in using Arrowsmith's translation was not to rewrite Seathl's speech, but simply to use some of the ideas and philosophy expressed in Arrowsmith's version. This film script is the basis for all the environmental versions attributed to Seathl. But there was one last phase the environmental version passed through. It was necessary to "shoehorn"[5] Perry's film script to meet the Baptists' religious and political agendas. John Stevens had been hired as a producer for the Baptists to do just that. He added all the references to God and "I am a savage and do not understand."

The first four chapters of this book focus on the original version of the speech by Smith. In Chapter I, I give a brief account of Seathl's life. In the second chapter I sketch the lives of Smith and Stevens, why they crossed paths and the exact date the speech may have been given. The third chapter is an attempt to answer the question: Why the thirty-three year lapse between the time Seathl spoke and Smith's publishing of the speech? The fourth chapter is a comparison of Smith's version and the only other recorded speeches by Seathl, two recorded by government interpreters and the other by someone who spoke Chinook jargon fluently. I compare these three speeches with Smith's noting the differences in the use of metaphors and similes and the similarity of style of the three speeches when compared to Smith's version. The fifth chapter deals with Bagley's and Rich's alterations of the speech and who may have been the first to unearth Smith's original version. The information in all of these five chapters is gleaned from a mixture of diaries, memoirs, old newspaper accounts, the research done by others and in the case of Seathl, interviews given by contemporaries who knew him.

The last two chapters focus on the environmental versions of the speech. At the time I began the research all of the people who were involved with the environmental speech in one way or the other were still alive so much my information is based on letters and telephone interviews. Arrowsmith died twenty-three years ago, and John Steven

---

[5] John Stevens, interview by the author, 30 April 1995, Sebastopol, California, telephone. Hereafter cited in the text as Stevens, 30 April 1995.

died in 2012. As of this writing only Ted Perry is alive. I am also indebted to those who have published their own research regarding the environmental speech.

My intention in writing this is to compile the history of the many speeches attributed to Chief Seathl and to try to shed some light as to why so many people altered his speech to meet their own agenda. I also wanted to gather all the research done by others, establish the fact the speech was spoken, and give an accurate account of the history of the environmental speech. No one has attempted to bring all these variations of the speech together and this is the only account that all three men responsible for the environmental version agree is an accurate account of what happened.

Chapter 1

The Life of Chief Seathl

In January of 1854, on the shores of the Puget Sound, Chief Seathl [6] of the Suquamish Nation purportedly gave a prophetic environmental speech to Governor Isaac Ingalls Stevens. In this speech, noted for its respect and compassion for life,[7] Seathl said:

> One thing we know, which the white man may one day discover--our God is the same God.
> You may think now that you own Him as you wish to own our land; but you cannot. He is the God of man, and His compassion is equal for the red man and the white.[8]

Seathl, however, never spoke these words. John Stevens, a producer for the Southern Baptist Convention Radio and Television Commission,

---

[6]Chief Seathl, Sealth or Sealt is commonly and incorrectly spelled Seattle. This was "the name of his father's father at a grand potlatch." David Buerge, "The Man We Call Seattle," *The Seattle Weekly*, 29 June 1983, 24. Hereafter cited in the text as Buerge, "We Call Seattle." For a more detailed discussion of this matter see Appendix 13.

[7]*The Pioneer (Olympia, Washington)*, 11 January 1854, 1. David M. Buerge, "Seattle's King Arthur: How Chief Seattle continues to inspire his many admirers to put words in his mouth," *The Seattle Weekly*, 17 July 1991, 28. Hereafter cited in the text as Buerge, "Seattle's King Arthur."

[8]This paragraph was among a number of additions written by John Stevens to the original script written by Ted Perry. Ted Perry, *Home*, ed. John Stevens, (Dallas, Texas: Southern Baptist Radio and Television Commission, 1971). Hereafter cited in the text as Stevens, *Home*. For a more detailed discussion of this matter see Chapter VI, Appendix 7 and Appendix 8.

wrote these words in 1971 despite the claim by the Southern Baptist Convention Radio and Television Commission that they were the words of Seathl. What Chief Seathl may have said was:

> Your God loves your people and hates mine; he folds his strong arms around the white man and leads him as a father leads his infant son, but he has forsaken his red children; . . . The white man's God cannot love his red children or he would protect them.[9]

This version, however, is also questionable. Dr. Henry Allen Smith wrote the passage from notes he said he took while Seathl spoke.[10] Thirty-three years later Smith transcribed his notes into the speech and published it in the October 29, 1887, edition of the *Seattle Sunday Star*. But no one has ever seen those notes except the elders of the Suquamish Nation.[11]

In the last forty-five years, the environmental version of Seathl's speech has spread far beyond the "Green" movement. Countless people, in many newspapers, magazine articles and books have repeated this speech. People use words from the environmental version on logos, bumper stickers, buttons and t-shirts. The speech was widely disseminated in Europe. In the 1970s and 80s numerous European ecological parties, including the German Green Party, used Seathl's speech to lend credibility to the environmental movement. The speech's widespread interest in Europe caught the attention of a German professor of Native American Studies, Rudolph Kaiser. In a 1987 essay he documented his research.

> There may hardly be a country in Western Europe where Seattle's speech has not been published in

---

[9]Dr. Henry A. Smith, "Early Reminiscences Number Ten, Scraps From A Diary," *Seattle Sunday Star*, 29 October 1887, 7. Hereafter cited in the text as Smith, *Seattle Star*.

[10]At the end of "Early Reminiscences Number Ten, Scraps From A Diary," Smith wrote that "other speakers followed [Seathl], but I took no notes." Smith, *Seattle Star*, 7. For a more detailed discussion of this matter see Appendix 1.

[11] The author spoke with Marilyn Jones of the Suquamish Nation who said according to their traditions Dr. Smith consulted the tribal elders numerous times before publishing the speech in the local paper in 1887. She also said the elders saw the notes Dr. Smith took while he listened to Seathl speak to Governor Stevens. Jones, 14 September 2007. For a more detailed discussion of this matter see Appendix 14.

> translation and hailed as a document of exemplary
> ecological sentiment. . . . Many schools and other
> educational institutions in Europe teach courses on
> ecological issues that frequently make use of a film . . .
> [which] consists solely of Chief Seattle's
> [environmental] speech.[12]

European radio programs, a German missionary order and the London based United Society for the Propagation of the Gospel have also used the speech.[13] In the PBS documentary, *The Power of Myth*, Bill Moyers interviewed Joseph Campbell, who read the "environmental speech" citing Chief Seathl as the author. Campbell made the common error of referring to it as a letter.[14]

Despite the lofty ideals attributed to him, Seathl never spoke about ecology and the environment; he never prophesied the inevitable destruction of the earth by the white man and never spoke of God's love for the red man. Many of the authors who edited the environmental versions are unknown, but we know some of those who edited earlier versions of Seathl's speech.

Those individuals who have manipulated the speech over the last 128 years had clear intentions to use Seathl to authenticate their own particular social, religious or political movement. This book attempts to identify five major stages through which the speech passed and the motives that may have led the authors to rewrite the speech.

The first stage was Dr. Henry A. Smith's 1887 published account of Seathl's speech and the 1891 reprint of Smith's version by a

---

[12] Rudolf Kaiser, "Chief Seattle's Speech(es): American Origins and European Reception" in *Recovering the Word*, ed., Brian Swann and Arnold Krupat (Berkeley: University of California Press, 1987), 500 & 497. Hereafter cited in the text as Kaiser, "Seattle's Speech(es)." "It is precisely this great number of publications which makes it impossible to mention them all." Ibid.

[13]Ibid., 499.

[14]The National Archives "concluded that the letter. . . is probably spurious." Richard C. Crawford of the Natural Resources Branch of the Civil Archives Division of the National Archives and Records Service, 2 November 1976, to E. Nolan of the Seattle Historical Society in response to Nolan's inquiry as to the authenticity of the "letter," Richard C. Crawford, Washington D.C., to E. Nolan, Seattle, Washington, 2 November 1976. Transcript at The Museum of History and Industry, Seattle, Washington. Joseph Campbell, *Power of Myth*, Interview by Bill Moyers, ed., Betty Sue Flowers (New York: Doubleday, 1988), 33-5.

Puget Sound historian, Frederic Grant. Seathl never spoke in the Victorian verbiage found in Smith's transcription. What is uncertain is how much if any of Smith's words reflect the thoughts and ideas that Seathl was conveying. The thirty-three year gap between Smith's publication and the day Seathl's spoke may reflect a political agenda on Smith's part. When Smith published the speech, the Puget Sound was in the midst of considerable economic and political turmoil. In an astounding upset, the citizens who had recently emigrated to the area in the 1870s and early 1880s unseated the original pioneers in the municipal and county elections of 1887. These pioneers had been in power for over thirty-three years. When Seathl spoke to the pioneers in 1854, was he expressing his own foreboding as he looked into the future of his people and their ancestral grounds? Or was Smith using Seathl as a mouthpiece in 1887 to express his own foreboding as he looked into the future of Seattle? There are no clear answers to these questions.

The next stage was in the late 1920's and early 1930's. It was the beginning of significant adulterations to Smith's text. A well-known Puget Sound historian, Clarence B. Bagley, and a local dentist, John M. Rich, both published their versions of the speech within years of each other. They loosely followed Smith's text, but Bagley, for instance, made some sort of editorial change in at least eighty percent of Smith's sentences. Rich also changed the text to suit his romantic fantasies of Native Americans and their role in our culture. Seathl was merely a vehicle for Rich's social commentary; a sad truth that would often be repeated in the late twentieth century.

The third stage was a translation of Smith's Victorian verbiage. In 1969 William Arrowsmith, a professor of Classical Studies, read Smith's text and attempted to rewrite it in a way that might reflect a sense of how Seathl spoke that day. Arrowsmith never claimed that his version was an accurate translation of Seathl's words. In fact, by the late 1980's he thought that Smith had completely fabricated the text.

The birth of the environmental version, the fourth stage, was in 1970 when a friend of Arrowsmith's, Ted Perry, wrote a film script loosely based on Arrowsmith's translation. At the time, Perry was an assistant professor of Theatre Arts at the same university where Arrowsmith worked: the University of Texas. He never claimed his text was the words of Seathl. He "invented a fictious Native American speech with more emphasis on the environment, and used it for a soundtrack on the film I [Perry] was working on. . ."[15] Although the film script was filled with warnings of environmental devastation if the white man continued their destructive ways, there were no statements of the redmen being savages or of religiosity. These were to come in the final phase: the fifth stage.

Perry had a contract with the Southern Baptist Radio and Television Commission to write three scripts of his choice. The first film script was his first and last. The producer, John Stevens, was the person responsible for adding the religiosity and "I am a savage and do not understand." Stevens' job was to edit films and "adapt them to meet the agenda and interests of the Southern Baptists Radio and Television Commission."[16] He also removed in the credits "written by Ted Perry" and replaced it with "adapted from a speech by Chief Seathl." All the subsequent environmental speeches or letters that purportedly came from Seathl are based on this edited film script. And all are far removed from Smith's original version of Seathl's speech.

Although there is no way to authenticate Smith's transcription of the meeting between Chief Seathl and Governor Stevens, there are documents verifying Stevens' visit to Seattle and his meeting with the Native Americans. On January 10, 1854, Governor Stevens sailed on the *Sarah Stone,* a small sailboat or "plunger," to tour the Puget Sound. Stevens wrote that his purpose was "to visit and take a census of the Indian tribes, learn something of the general character of the Sound and its harbors."[17] He wrote of stopping at the future site of Seattle and seeing "a large body of Indians of nearly all the tribes."[18] At the time of Stevens' visit, Seathl was the most powerful chief in the area. There can be little doubt that Seathl greeted Governor Stevens as Dr. Smith stated. Only four years before, Seathl had greeted the first Americans to land at his village. One of these Americans recorded Seathl's

---

[15]Ted Perry to the author, 25 October 1991. Transcript at Eli Gifford, Sebastopol, California and The Seattle Museum of History and Industry, Seattle, Washington. Hereafter cited in the text as Perry, 25 October 1991. For a more detailed discussion of this matter see Appendix 7 and Appendix 8.

[16] Stevens, 30 April 1995.

[17]Hazard Stevens, *The Life of Isaac Ingalls Stevens,* vol. 1 (New York: Houghton, Mifflin and Co., 1901), 1:416-7. Hereafter cited in the text as Stevens, *Life of Stevens.* Stevens used no footnotes or endnotes. He merely listed his sources at the beginning of the book. For a detailed list of his sources see Appendix 8.

[18]Stevens, *Life of Stevens,* 416-7.

greeting. While Seathl spoke to Stevens, Smith took notes and later transcribed them into the speech published in the October 29, 1887, edition of the *Seattle Sunday Star.*

When Governor Stevens sailed down the Puget Sound, Chief Seathl was in his late fifties or early sixties.[19] He was the son of a Suquamish[20] chief, Schweabe, whose people lived on islands across the Puget Sound from present day Seattle.[21] His mother, Scholitza,[22] was

---

[19] Seathl was born sometime between 1786-1790 and died on June 7, 1866. Vanderwerth believes he was born in 1786. W.C. Vanderwerth, ed., *Indian Oratory*, with a foreword by William R. Carmack (Norman: University of Oklahoma Press, 1971), 117. Hereafter cited in the text as Vanderwerth, *Oratory*. David Buerge, the foremost scholar of Seathl, also agrees with the date 1786. Buerge, "Seattle's King Arthur," 27. Bagley believes Seathl was born in 1790. Clarence B. Bagley, *History of Seattle: From the Earliest Settlements to the Present Time*, vol. 1 (Chicago: S.J. Clarke Publishing Co., 1916), 78. Hereafter cited in the text as Bagley, *History of Seattle*. Clarence Bagley was a noted Pacific Northwest historian at the turn of the century. According to Buerge, "the best biography of him [Seathl, is], a monograph written by Clarence Bagley in 1931, is not widely known, and the author did not have access to much reliable ethnographic material." Buerge, "We Call Seattle," 24.

[20] There is some confusion as to the name of his tribe in some early writings. For instance Suquamps is written on Seathl's gravestone, Sokwamish is the name used by Puget Sound missionaries found in the "The Letters of the Quebec Missionaries" - from 1838 on . . . although in another letter it was spelled Sockwamish or Sukwampsh. A. Felix Verwilgen, "Chief Sealth In the Letters of the First Christian Missionairies of the Puget Sound Area," May 1964, 1. Transcript at The Museum of History and Industry, Seattle, Washington. Lucile McDonald, "Was Tslalakom Real Name of Chief Sealth?," *The Seattle Times, Sunday*, 2 August 1964, 6. Hereafter cited in the text as McDonald, "Tslalakom." But there is no tribe by the name of Suquamps or Sokwamish in the *Handbook of North American Indians Vol .7 Northwest Coast*. There is a Pacific coast tribe called Skokomish and according to tradition Seathl's father was constantly at the war with them. Frank Carlson, *Chief Sealth* Bulletin Series III No. 2 (Seattle: University of Washington, December 1903), 14. Hereafter cited in the text as Carlson, *Chief Sealth.*

[21] Each village was divided into a number of large house groups each associated with a chief and retainers who were the immediate family, slaves and commoners. "Rank of chief or noble is connected in most cases with a certain degree of personal power, but real communal authority is naturally vested in only the highest chief or chiefs of the village, and then not always as absolute as we are inclined to imagine." Edward Sapir, "The Social Organization of the West Coast Tribes" from the Transaction of the Royal Society of Canada Series III 1915 Vol. IX (Ottawa: Printed for the Royal Society of Canada 1915). Presented by Dr. Adam Shorff (Read May Meeting 1915) 360.

Duwamish and a concubine of Schweabe making Seathl the son of a slave. Lines of descent were matrilineal so Seathl was Duwamish. Despite his low birth, Seathl was renowned as a warrior noted for his courage, daring, leadership and diplomacy.

He became chief in his early twenties after defeating a war party of a hundred warriors about to attack his village. These warriors were from the mountain tribes of the upper Green and White Rivers in the Cascades. Word had reached Seathl's tribe that the war party was planning a raid on his village and the surrounding saltwater tribes.[23] These mountain tribes were known for their ferocity and had attacked and defeated the saltwater tribes before, carrying off many people for slaves. The chiefs from the saltwater tribes held a council. None of the plans for defeating the raiding party were satisfactory. The chiefs then turned to the young warriors for counsel. Seathl was the first among the warriors to speak. His strategy was so superior to what had been presented that the council adopted it immediately.[24] When the plan successfully routed the war party, the council declared Seathl chief.

---

[22]Or Woodsholitsa. Frederick J. Dockstader, *Great North American Indians Profiles in Life and Leadership* (San Francisco: Van Nostrand Reinhold Co., 1977), 258. Hereafter cited in the text as Dockstader, *American Indian Profiles*. Bagley, *History of Seattle*, 78.

[23]The saltwater tribes were those villages living on the Puget Sound and surrounding islands.

[24]His plan was to block the Green River as the war party floated down. There was a sharp bend in the river where the current was swift. Just downstream from the bend were rapids. At the bend Seathl had a large pine tree felled. It took nearly a day to chop it down and position it, but when it was ready it was just a few inches above the water making it impossible for the canoes to go under it. Seathl hid his warriors on either side of the banks. When the first war canoes came around the bend they capsized and were ambushed by the hidden warriors. Hearing the cries of battle, the war party still upstream beached their canoes and hurried back home bringing word of defeat. The rapids are "near what is now Longacres Racetrack," Buerge, "We Call Seattle," 24. Sam Coombs believes the attack took place "on the White river, near where John Fountain now lives above the Black river bridge . . ." The story of Seathl's exploits is based on interviews conducted by Coombs with "several of the oldest natives" in the summer of 1860. Sam Coombs was an early pioneer of the Puget Sound and his reminiscences are the basis of most of the early descriptions of Seathl. J.A. Costello, *The Siwash Their Life Legends and Tales: Puget Sound and Pacific Northwest* (Seattle: Calvert Co., 1895), 103. Hereafter cited in the text as Costello, *Life Legends and Tales*. Also in S.F. Coombs, "Good Chief Seattle: How a Young Warrior Became Ruler of Many Tribes," *Post-Intelligencer(Seattle)*, 26 March 1893, 1. Hereafter cited in the text as Coombs, "Good Chief Seattle."

A grand council of the tribes was called, composed of the chiefs and leading warriors and medicine men from the following six tribes: Old-Man-House, Moxliepush, Duwamish, Black River, Shilshole and Lake, whose chiefs were Kitsap, Seattle Curley, Tecumseh, Salmon Bay Curley and Lake John, Seattle Curley being chief of both the Moxliepush and the Duwamish tribes. At this council Sealth was made great chief of all tribes and the former chiefs became typees, or sub-chiefs. The Moxliepush, Black River and Lake tribes, however, did not consent.[25]

Seathl gathered his most fearless warriors and set out to subjugate the three tribes who refused to acquiesce to his authority as the great chief. Through diplomacy and oratory, he won over the recalcitrant tribes. After uniting these three tribes, he made treaties with the other surrounding villages. He also stopped the raiding from the tribes further to the north and south. In a short time, Seathl had not only expanded the territory of the Suquamish, but also his influence and control.[26]

The first written record of Seathl appears in Dr. William Frazer Tolmie's diary. Tolmie was the surgeon at the Hudson's Bay Company post on the Nisqually Prairie, Fort Nisqually.[27] During the building of the fort in the summer of 1833,[28] Tolmie wrote a description of Seathl, "a brawny Suquamish with Roman countenance and black curley [*sic*]

[25]Coombs, "Good Chief Seattle" 1.

[26] For a more detailed discussion on the use of oral traditions for historical documentation see Appendix 14. Ezra Meeker wrote in his *Pioneer Reminiscences* that "Se-ath of Seattle, as he was afterwards known, was reported to be the chief of six tribes or band, but at best this control was like most all the chiefs on the [Puget] Sound but shadowy." Ezra Meeker, *Frontier Reminiscences of the Puget Sound* (Chicago: Library Resources, 1970; Library of American civilization microfiche), 180, LAC 13265. Hereafter cited in the text as Meeker, *Reminiscences*. Also Costello, *Life Legends and Tales*, 104; Coombs, "Good Chief Seattle," 2; Carlson, *Chief Sealth*, 8; Buerge, " We Call Seattle," 24.

[27]". . . he is remembered chiefly as superintendent of the Puget Sound Agricultural Company." Cecil Dryden, *Dryden's History of Washington* (Portland Oregon: 1968), 188. Hereafter cited in the text as Dryden, *Dryden's History*.

[28]John S. Galbraith, *The Hudson's Bay Company As an Imperial Factor 1821-1869* (Berkeley: University of California Press, 1957), 203. Hereafter cited in the text as Galbraith, *Hudson's Bay Company*.

hair, handsomest Indian I ever saw."[29] Soon after Tolmie wrote this entry Seathl was banned for a short time from the post for his belligerent attitude.[30] Seathl was about forty-six years old at this time.

The relationship between Fort Nisqually and the Native Americans was primarily an economic one. However, Dr. Tolmie and Francis Heron, an employee in charge of building the fort, taught basic Christian practices to the local indigenous population. The company's interest in the Native Americans' moral character actually stems back to 1821 when the Company reorganized and the royal license required "religious instruction and moral improvement of the Indians."[31] Tolmie's first act when he took charge of Nisqually was to discontinue the practice of fur trading on Sunday. He wrote in his diary, "I explained the creation of the world and the reason why Christians and Jews abstained from work on Sunday . . . the Indians could not comprehend things clearly."[32] Catholic Iroquois, employed by the Company, also began spreading Christian beliefs among the natives. In an attempt to bring civilization to the tribes, Heron and Dr. Tolmie gathered the headmen of the local tribes and had them sign an agreement "to end the practice of revenge murder." Seathl was one of the headmen to place his mark.[33]

His Christian conversion may be responsible for the metamorphosis from the belligerent war chief banned from Fort Nisqually to a pacific Christian leader.[34] On November 24, 1838, Father Francis Norbert Blanchet of the Montreal diocese and Father Modeste Demers from the Red River in Canada arrived at Fort Vancouver.[35] Father Blanchet became the vicar general for the

---

[29]Dr. Tolmie, *Journal of Occurences* at Nisqually House, quoted in Buerge, *We Call Seattle*, 24.

[30]Buerge, *We Call Seattle*, 25; "Chief Seattle and Angeline," *The Washington Historical Quarterly* (Vol. 22; 1931): 245. Hereafter cited in the text as Bagley, "Angeline."

[31]Quoted in Dryden, *Dryden's History*, 184.

[32]Robert Cantwell, *The Hidden Northwest* (New York: J.B. Lippinnott Co., 1972), 88. Hereafter cited in the text as Cantwell, *Hidden Northwest*. Dryden, *Dryden's History*, 184.

[33]Buerge, "We Call Seattle," 24-5.

[34]Costello, *Life Legends and Tales*, 105; Dockstader, *American Indian Profiles*, 258.

[35]They had traveled 5,325 miles. Oscar Osburn Winther, *The Great Northwest: A History*, 2nd ed. (New York: Alfred A. Knopf, 1960), 119. Hereafter cited in the text as Winther, *The Great Northwest*.

Northwest and in charge of the Oregon mission.[36] He established a mission in the Willamette Valley and his assistant Father Demers took charge of the Cowlitz Mission just south of the Puget Sound.[37] When the priests arrived in Oregon Territory, local Indians and French-Canadian *voyageurs* were "latent congregations awaiting them . . . most people had been long out of contact with their church, the priests were busy from the moment they arrived baptizing, solemnizing marriages, hearing confessions, celebrating Mass, and teaching prayers and catechisms."[38] Father Demers made several trips visiting the local tribes. Up to three thousand Native Americans may have attended these meetings. Demers baptized seven hundred and sixty-five Native Americans and during one of his visits he may have baptized Seathl giving him the baptismal name of Noah.[39] Although there is no conclusive evidence supporting baptism of Seathl by Father Demers, Seathl was a practicing Catholic holding morning and evening prayers by the early 1840s.[40]

Father Verwilghen, who wrote a paper documenting Seathl's relationship with the Catholics,[41] believes that Father Demers and Father Blanchet also called Chief Seathl by another name Chief Tslakom in their letters to the Diocese of Quebec.[42] Father Blanchet had preached in Tslakom's village in May-June 1840 and "he cannot yet have been baptized at that time."[43] Historian Frederick J. Dockstader

---

[36]At this time Washington Territory was still part of the Oregon Territory and jointly occupied by both the United States and Great Britain. Washington Territory was not established until 1853.

[37]Galbraith, *Hudson's Bay Company*, 204; Dryden, *Dryden's History*, 101.

[38]D.W. Meinig, *The Great Columbia Plain: A Historical Geography, 1805-1910* (Seattle: University of Washington Press, 1968), 142. Hereafter cited in the text as Meinig, *Columbia Plain.*

[39]On Chief Seathl's gravestone at Suquamish is engraved Noah Sealth. McDonald, "Tslalakom," 6. "[Seattle] had recently been baptised by the Roman Catholic priest, Father Modeste Demers [before Febuary, 1852]." Cantrell, *Hidden Northwest*, 95; Bagley, *History of Seattle*; quoted in *The Catholic North West Progress*, 18 December 1964, vol. 67, No. 51, 9. Father Verwilghen believes Seathl was baptized in his own village by Father Francis N. Blanchet in May or June, 1840. McDonald, "Tslalakom, " 6.

[40]Buerge, "We Call Seattle," 25.

[41]The paper was presented at The Pioneer Association of the State of Washington on May 1964.

[42]For a more detailed discussion of this matter see Appendix 13.

[43]Father Verwilghen, CICM, "Chief Sealth ca. 1786-1866 In the Letters of the first Christian Missionaries of the Puget Sound Area," presented by James Vernon

believes that the Catholic priests are largely responsible for Seathl renouncing war in the 1840s and following the path of peace among the Northwest tribes.[44] While there may be some truth to the priests' effect on Seathl, one of the foremost scholars on Chief Seathl's life, David Buerge, believes that there were other underlying reasons for Seathl's conversion:

> While Seattle's conversion was no doubt sincere, it had practical advantages. Through it he was able to cultivate relations with the whites who were the principal dispensers of metal, cloth, and guns. Many native leaders, however, were opposed to the activities of the priests and the presence of the whites altogether, so Seattle's support of both was not without risk. . . .
>
> His gradual change may have been more to do with his gradual emergence as an elder amongst his people, a position in which tact and diplomacy were more valued than the arts of war.[45]

Seathl was not the only leader to see the advantages of conversion. It "appears that interest that Balanchet and Demirs encountered was in part the result of the political use Salish leaders were finding in the new rituals and rules."[46]

Seven years after Father Demers took charge of the Cowlitz Mission, Americans began to settle the area around Puget Sound. The first Americans were a small party of men led by Michael Troutman Simmons who arrived in the spring of 1845 and built homesteads in the area.[47] These men were the forerunners of a flood of Americans

---

Metcalfe for the Pioneer Association of the State of Washington, May 1964, Museum of History and Industry, Seattle, Washington, 3.

[44]Dockstader, *American Indian Profiles*, 258.

[45]Buerge, "We Call Seattle," 25.

[46]Meinig, *Columbia Plain*, 500.

[47]Cantwell, *Hidden Northwest*, 18-9. Mary W. Avery, *History and Government of the State of Washington* (Seattle: University of Washington Press, 1961), 158-9. Hereafter cited in the text as Avery, *History and Government*. The first Americans to spend time in the area were two Yankee traders, Captain John Kendrick and Captain Robert Gray. Some Boston merchants found themselves at a disadvantage in trading with the Orient because manufactured Americans goods were inferior to the English goods.

who would soon not only overwhelm the small British population in the Puget Sound, but ultimately lead to the subjugation and demise of the native peoples. This deluge of Americans began in the early 1840s and became known as "Oregon Fever."

Until 1842 the settlers and the Native Americans in the Oregon Territory led a peaceful existence. The settlements were small and focused on the lower Columbia and Willamette valleys. European diseases devastated the tribes in these valleys and the surrounding areas so the Native Americans posed little threat to the settlers.[48] The tribes to the north, south and east however, were hostile and strong, but for the most part stayed within their own borders. A second reason for the peace among settlers and the indigenous population was that the

---

They hired Kendrick and Gray to trade American goods with the Northwest Indians for furs and then take the furs to the Orient. Captain Gray first set anchor with his ship *Columbia* just south of the Columbia River in August, 1788. In September 1789 the two met at Nootka on Vancouver Island. Kendrick stayed and Gray sailed for China returning to Boston in 1790 becoming the first American to circumnavigate the globe carrying the American flag. James Gilchrist Swan, *The Northwest Coast or, Three Years' Residence in Washington Territory* (New York: Harper & Row Publishers, 1857; reprint, New York: J.&J. Harper Editions, 1969), 126-132. Hereafter cited in the text as Swan, *Northwest Coast;* Sidney Warren, *Farthest Frontier: The Pacific Northwest* (London: Kennikat, 1949), 2-3. Hereafter cited in the text as Warren, *Farthest Frontier.*

[48]"As we know the Indian population in most regions declined drastically after contact with whites, principally because it had not adjusted physiologically and culturally after contact to the impact of new diseases." H.B. Hawthorn, C.S. Belshaw, S. M. Damieson, *The Indian of British Columbia: A Study of Contemporary Social Adjustment* (Toronto: University of Toronto, 1960), 22. All of the following quotes are from Robin Fischer, *Contact and Conflict: Indian-European Relations in British Columbia, 1774-1890* (Vancouver: University of British Columbia, 1977), 45. Reports of outbreaks of diseases among the Indians became more frequent in the 1830's. So were ". . . comments about 'dreadful ravages' of smallpox taking 'great numbers' of Indians. But the evidence is seldom more specific. Douglas wrote in 1838 that smallpox killed 1/3 of the population on the Northern Coast, but Reverend Herbert Beaver who wrote the following day, claimed that the disease had only taken one in three of those attacked." [Douglas to Simpson, 18 Mar. 1838, Rich, *Mcloughlin's Letter, First Series,* (London: Hudson's Bay Record Society, 1825-1828, 1941) p. 271; Beaver to Benjamin Harrison, 19 Mar. 1838, in Thomas Jessett, ed., *Reports and Letters of Herbert Beaver 1836-1838* (Portland, Oregon: Champeog Press, 1957) 88]. "All such estimates have to be treated with caution, particularly when based on Indian reports. Dr. William Tolmie, who by profession took great interest in the incidence of disease, claimed that experience had taught him to place little faith in the Indian accounts of the severity of the outbreaks because of their tendency to exaggerate misfortune." [William Fraser Tolmie, *Journals of W. F. Tolmie: Physician and Fur Trader* (Vancouver: Mitchell Press 1963)].

Hudson's Bay Company administrators knew how to deal with the latter. The Native Americans wanted to trade. The Company demanded that to trade they had to follow Company regulations and remain at peace. "The British at Fort Vancouver flogged natives who committed depredations and made it a point to apprehend such culprits to the degree that capture and punishment were sure."[49] The Native Americans had less respect for the Americans than the British because the former worked in the fields whereas the British used Indian labor. The Americans also had a reputation for "unprovoked attacks on natives, which was not true of the British."[50]

Tensions grew between the Native Americans and the settlers in the 1840s, as the settlers invaded the middle reaches of the Columbia valleys and emigrants passed through the eastern tribes' land in greater numbers. The emigrants brought disease and death. The Native Americans' anger only increased as more Americans arrived demanding land they considered property of the United States.

It was not until 1851 that the effects of the "Oregon Fever" reached the land surrounding Seathl's village. On November 13, 1851, the first pioneer families made their homes near Seathl's village. David Denny had arrived early in the fall with four other men to look for a site to found a city. In November he brought his wife and a group of twelve adults and twelve children.[51] The year before, Seathl welcomed a group of American explorers led by Issac Ebey.[52] Benjamin F. Shaw was among the party, but was "a mere boy." He wrote that Seathl "had with him a young Indian for an interpreter, as he could not speak the Chinook language. . . . As neither gentlemen could speak Chinook it

---

[49]Ray Hoard Glassley, *Indian Wars of the Pacific Northwest* (City unknown: By the author, 1953; reprint, Portland: Binfords & Mort, 1972), 2. Hereinafter cited as Glassley, *Indian Wars.* "The Hudson's Bay Company have no false, romantic ideas of Indians, or that bogus species of philanthropy. . . They look upon an Indian simply as he is a wild savage, but a man who has rights which they take care to respect." Swan, *Northwest Coast,* 375.

[50]Glassley, *Indian Wars,* 2.

[51] Cantwell, *Hidden Northwest,* 95; Avery, *History and Government,* 159-60; they "confidently called the place 'New York.' However, growth was much slower than they had expected, so it seemed fitting to affix a Chinook Jargon word 'Alki,' meaning 'by and by.'" Dryden, *Dryden's History,* 116.

[52]Ebey was one of the first pioneers to settle Whidbey Island on the Sound. Cantrell, *Hidden Northwest,* 97; Avery, *History and Government,* 159.

fell to my lot to answer him [Seathl]."⁵³ This greeting was Seathl's earliest recorded speech:

> My name is Sealt and this great swarm of people that you see are my people; they have come down here to celebrate the coming of the first run of good salmon. As the salmon are our chief food we always rejoice to see them coming early and in abundance, for this insures [*sic*] us a plentiful quantity of food for the coming winter. This is the reason our hearts are glad today, and so you do not want to take this wild demonstration as warlike. It is meant in the nature of a salute in imitation of the Hudson's Bay Company's salute to their chiefs when they arrive at Victoria. I am glad to have you come to our country, for we Indians know but little and you Boston and King George men know how to do every thing [*sic*]. We want your blankets, your guns, axes, clothing, tobacco, and all other things you make. We need all these things that you make, as we do not know how to make them, and so we welcome you to our country to make flour, sugar and other things that we can trade for. We wonder why the Boston men should wander so far away from their

⁵³"Though a man of great natural abilities, Chief Sealth never learned either Chinook or the English languages; nor did the older Indians whom I knew." Sam Coombs quoted in Costello, *Life Legends and Tales*, 105. In a letter to Clarence Bagley, Wells Drury, the official interpreter for the first Puget Sound Indian agent, Rev. Alfred Elder, wrote of Seathl's linguistic abilities. Elder wanted his ten-year-old nephew, Drury, to be his interpreter, but there was much disagreement because of his age. So it came down to a panel of judges to decide which of the three applicants spoke Chinook well enough to become the interpreter. Seathl was one of the judges. "Seattle grunting out that I was entirely too young . . . Seattle didn't like to speak Chinook . . . After a year's practice I placated Seattle by talking to him in his own dialect." After quoting this Bagley added "In all the biographies of Chief Seattle, including my own, it has been represented that he did not understand Chinook Jargon. The foregoing shows that this is not correct. He and all of the older Indians did not like the Jargon, nor did they use it among themselves." Bagley, "Angeline," 261-2. The Northwest Indians "appear to have a great aversion to learning the English language, contenting themselves with the Jargon, which they look upon as a sort of white man's talk. They, however, are not so averse to learning French, probably because they can imitate the sounds of French words easier that they can the English." Swan, *Northwest Coast*, 317.

home and come among so many Indians. Why are you not afraid?[54]

Since this translation is "probably the most accurate translation of Seattle's remarks"[55] it is important to note Seathl's style of speaking, his syntax and the words found in this greeting to determine the authenticity of his other purported speeches. Three years later, Seathl spoke with Governor Stevens. The meeting between Seathl and Stevens was the basis of Dr. Smith's version of the speech. But the words in Seathl's greeting to Isaac Ebey and his group of explorers are probably one of the more accurate because Benjamin Shaw recorded it directly from Chinook jargon.[56] Shaw "was alleged to be the only man in the territory who could translate from English into Chinook tongue while a man talked a normal speed."[57] "Colonel B. F. Shaw . . . spoke the language fluently."[58] Shaw's recording "is then probably the most accurate translation of Seattle's remarks in English that could be made after they had passed through the jargon."[59] Shaw's linguistic abilities were so well respected that four years later he was Governor Stevens'

---

[54] Clarence Bagley, *Bagley's Scrapbook*, No.11 Special Collections, University of Washington, Seattle. Hereafter cited in the text as Bagley, *Bagley's Scrapbook*. Buerge, "We Call Seattle," 25. There are no records of any sub-chiefs greeting the Americans.

[55] Buerge, "We Call Seattle," 25.

[56] A trade language of five hundred words, which was a mixture of English and the local native languages. It was used among the Northwest Indians and whites. George Gibbs wrote in his book *Dictionary of the Chinook Jargon or Trade Language of Oregon* that by the time it was published in 1865 "many formerly employed [words] have become in great measure obsolete while other have been locally introduced. . . . Some terms in Dalles of the Columbia would not be intelligible at Astoria or in the Puget Sound. . . I have included all those which on reference to a number of vocabularies I have found current at any of these places. . . . Total number of all a little short of five hundred words." George Gibbs, *Dictionary of the Chinook Jargon or Trade Language of Oregon*, (New York: Cramoisy Press, 1865; reprint, New York: AMS Press Inc., 1970), vii., (page reference is to reprint edition). Gibb's book is "the most authoritative. . . Gibbs. . . spent twelve years on the Northwest coast in the first half of the past century." Edward Harper Thomas, *Chinook: A History of the Northwest Coast Trade Jargon*, Portland: Metropolitan Press, Publishers, 1935), 3.

[57] Kent D. Richards, *Isaac I. Stevens: Young Man in A Hurry* (Provo, Utah: Brigham Young University Press, 1979.), 197. Hereafter cited in the text as Richards, *Stevens*. Buerge wrote that Shaw "was said to have been a master of the jargon and to have been able to speak the native languages as well." Buerge, "We Call Seattle," 25.

[58] Swan, *Northwest Coast*, 309.

[59] Buerge, "We Call Seattle," 25.

chief interpreter when Stevens traveled around the territory negotiating treaties with the tribes.

By the early 1850s many of the Northwest tribes were becoming more than dissatisfied with the rapid expansion of Americans. The encroachment of Americans had reached the point where the local Indians were in direct competition for land with the invaders.

> Beginning in 1850 tribes, which had previously caused little or no concern, became restless. People talked about it, editors wrote about it, army officers tried to analyze it. No doubt the sight of increasing numbers of settlers revealed to the Indians the end of their free control of the wide-open spaces.[60]

This was the environment in which Seathl gave his speech in January of 1854 to Governor Stevens.

By 1854 hostility had increased to the point where several settlers and local tribesmen had been killed. In 1855 it exploded into a war between the Washington tribes and settlers. This war had many roots. "The disruption brought upon the Puget Sound and Columbia River tribes by dispossession and removal, epidemics, white encroachment and government delays in ratification of the treaties had resulted . . . [in the] Puget Sound uprisings."[61] The devastating effects of the European diseases on the Indian populations provided another cause for the war. The first epidemic of smallpox attacked the Puget Sound area in 1830 to 1833.[62] For the settlers the greatest single

---

[60]Glassley, *Indian Wars*, 53.

[61]Cesare Marion, "History of Western Washington Since 1846," in *Handbook of North American Indians Vol. 7 Northwest Coast,* ed. William Sturtevant (Washington: Smithsonian Institute, 1990), 171. Hereafter cited in the text as Marion, "History of Washington."

[62]It has been estimated that the tribes in the Willamette valley were a tenth of what they were before 1829. "The one-tenth figure was McLoughlin's [in charge of all the Pacific operations for the Hudson's Bay Company] estimate; Parker suggested that probably seven-eighths had died. An excellent study of the epidemic which establishes its nature and extent is S.F. Cook, 'The Epidemic of 1830-1833 in California and Oregon,' *University of California Publications in American Archaelogy and Ethnology,* 43, No. 3 (1955), 303-26," quoted in Meinig, *Columbia Plain,* 122 and 123n; Buerge, "We Call Seattle," 24; Schwantes, *The Pacific Northwest,* 36-7.

problem was that the Native Americans were living on the best land. Many of the clearings were the result of the Native Americans' labor and the settlers were eager to file claims on the land occupied by the tribes.

The native populations responded to the pressures of the increasing white population, the technology of guns and the decimation of their tribes in a number of ways. They began kidnapping women and children from other tribes and warring over tribal land with far more frequency. It is uncertain whether warfare had increased during Seathl's generation, but among Seathl's "father's generation and his own, war leaders were the most prominent, and the peoples' memories of battles they fought does not seem to have gone back very far."[63] By 1852, the population of whites had reached a critical mass where they qualified for a territorial government.

Not only was there discontent among the Native Americans with so many whites invading their land, but between the settlers north and south of the Columbia River. Almost as soon as Oregon became a territory, the settlers in what was going to become the Territory of Washington claimed the Oregon capital was too far away. In 1851 they refused to allow the United States District Court to convene in Cowlitz Valley saying that their choice on the Chehalis River was "a spot selected by the county commissioners as the rightful seat of government. . . . The northerners felt under privileged. . . . Probably the heart of the matter was that the 'north-of-the-river' settlers needed more attention than they were receiving."[64] On August 29, 1851, the "northerners" held the Cowlitz Convention and adopted a memorial petitioning Congress for the creation of the "Territory of Columbia" (eventually to be named Territory of Washington). In November of 1852 the "northerners" sent the memorial to Congress and in its very next session the Oregon Territorial Legislature sent a petition

---

[63]Warfare in the 1800's was largely defensive. Villages were generally on good terms with their neighbors because of marriage and kinship. "There was no institution through which warriors could be mobilized and so fighting . . . did not develop into a more organized warfare.". Sam Coombs quoted in Costello, *Life Legends and Tales*, 105. In a period just before Lewis and Clark the inland tribes, hunters and horsemen, were expanding their range into territory previously held by the coast tribes . . . . Farther north in British Columbia and on Queen Charlotte Island, were the Haidas . . . whose raids into the Puget Sound were equally terrifying to the Indians and to the white settlers." Cantrell, *Hidden Northwest*, 137.

[64]Dryden, *Dryden's History*, 119; Meinig, *Columbia Plain*, 168-172.

recommending the same. Here Isaac Ingalls Stevens entered the picture.

Chapter II

The Story of

Dr. Henry A Smith, Governor Isaac I. Stevens

and the Meeting

Between Chief Seathl and Governor Stevens

Isaac I. Stevens had been an officer in the United States Army and fought in the Mexican War of 1846-1848. Upon returning to the States he helped administer the United States Coast and Geodetic Survey which included mapping shores and navigable rivers, lighthouse sites and identifying future navigational problems. During the Presidential election of 1852, the supporters of General Winfield Scott began to attack the military record of Franklin Pierce, the Democratic candidate. Stevens "was indignant at these slanders." He wrote six letters to support Pierce's presidential bid and Pierce's record in the Mexican War. The *Boston Post* published three of the letters, the *Republic* published three and a Washington D.C. paper published one. While still an officer in the Army, he gave several speeches in support of Pierce.[65] Political leaders warmly praised his defense of Pierce's war record. They said his speeches had "done much good."[66] As a result of his support for Pierce, Stevens knew "he could claim any reasonable political reward."[67] Stevens realized that success and power lay in

---

[65]Stevens, *Life of Stevens*, 272.
[66]Quoted in Richards, *Stevens*, 94.
[67]Ibid, 95.

politics, not in his military career. The California Gold Rush was only two years old and the West was rapidly expanding. "A man with ambition could gain for himself in a year what it might take decades or lifetimes to accomplish in the East. Stevens had no doubt about his ambitions, but he had been struggling to find a field of action broad enough for them."[68] Stevens also recognized "that with the army on a peace footing and filled with young officers, no promotion in his corps could be expected for years. . . . he was not content to remain longer a subordinate."[69]

On March 17, 1853, President Pierce appointed Stevens the first Governor of the newly formed Washington Territory. Along with the governorship came the Office of Superintendent of Indian Affairs for the Territory. This territory extended from the Rockies to the Pacific coast. But the real plum for Stevens was the command of the northern transcontinental railroad survey. As a general rule the politicians that filled territorial posts were noted for their mediocrity. There was little political power in these outposts and little chance for promotion. If he could persuade Congress to locate the Pacific terminus in Washington Territory, all of that would change for Stevens. The Pacific terminus guaranteed his territory would become a powerful economic force in the West.[70]

Stevens was a true believer in Manifest Destiny. To him, the local Indian populations impeded Western Civilization's advancement. "He assumed the superiority of European civilization and the necessity of removing the Indian from its path."[71] As far as he was concerned the Native Americans could only benefit from the American presence.

Stevens' analytical ability was well known. When faced with a problem he quickly broke it into components and found solutions for each. This served him well as a soldier in the Army and an administrator in the United States Coast and Geodetic Survey.[72] When he arrived in Washington Territory, he used these very same methods

---

[68]David M. Buerge, "Isaac the Terrible: A Portrait of an Extraordinary Pioneer and Brilliant Explorer, Heroic Adventurer and Reckless Ruler," *Weekly: Seattle's News Magazine*, 28 August, 1985 (Seattle: Sasquatch Publishing Co.), 25. Hereafter cited in the text as Buerge, "Isaac the Terrible."

[69]Stevens, *Life of Stevens*, 280.

[70]Ibid., 97.

[71]Richards, *Stevens*, 191.

[72]Stevens, *Life of Stevens*, 20-1; Richards, *Stevens*, 97.

when faced with the enormous task of making peace with the Native Americans in an area that stretched from Rockies to the Puget Sound. His goal was to sign peace treaties with all the tribes and to begin moving them onto a reservation within two years. This was an impossible timetable. His first move was dividing the Territory into seven districts, appointing Indian Agents for each and having them contact the chiefs in their districts. Ultimately, Stevens believed the best way to deal with the "native problem" was to concentrate all the tribes on reservations where acculturation could take place quickly. The very abilities that led to his success as a military man--his analytical abilities and his ability to lead soldiers--were the defects that brought the wrath of many settlers and led to the war with the Indians.[73]

> The insecure Stevens responded to independent minds [Washington settlers] or differing opinions with impatience or intransigence. Not surprisingly, difficulties in dealing with such people first manifested themselves during the Northern Survey.[74]

Stevens could not have misjudged the character of the Native Americans more. Their culture required deliberation and time to discuss all the aspects of the issue at hand. In this case it was selling their homeland and the land of their ancestors. As a people they were independent and not inclined to follow the edicts of Governor Stevens just because the "Great White Father" said so.

In 1850, Congress enacted a federal law to remove all the Northwest tribes from their homeland and relocate them east of the Cascades. A year after he arrived Governor Stevens asserted that the Indians looked forward to their demise:

---

[73]"His sense of being able to dominate problems by creating solutions combined with the inflexible determination he learned from his father, produced in Stevens a formidable will. His ability break down problems into their parts and organize their solutions was to serve him well as governor and planner. But they were to cause him grief in less tractable human situations where resolute determination looked like stubborn intransigence." Buerge, "Isaac the Terrible," 25.

[74]Ibid., 25.

> The speedy extinction of the race seems rather to be
> hoped for than regretted, and they look forward to it
> themselves with a sort of indifference.[75]

Clearly, he misunderstood and seriously miscalculated the Native Americans for whom he was responsible. Within a year of writing these words, Stevens would find himself in the middle of a war with a people who he had thought "hoped for [rather] than regretted . . ." their ". . . speedy extinction."

In his first year as governor, he spent most of his time in Washington D.C. getting funds for the new territory, lobbying for a northern railroad and arranging his family's move west. During his time away, the Indian agents prepared for the treaty councils. Stevens planned to negotiate and sign all treaties in the spring and summer of 1855. This included all the Native Americans from the saltwater tribes on the Puget Sound to the Native Americans in present day Montana.

> Not only was the [Stevens] timetable reckless; the
> whole enterprise was organized in profound ignorance
> of native society, culture, and history. The 20,000-odd
> aboriginal inhabitants, who were assumed to be in rapid
> decline were given a brutal choice: They could adapt to
> white society or they could disappear.[76]

---

[75]Department of Interior, Bureau of Indian Affairs, *Indian Tribes West of the Cascades*, by Isaac I. Stevens, open-file report, Annual Report of the Office of Indian Affairs (Wash., D.C., 1854), 453.

[76] Buerge, "Isaac the Terrible," 27. Stevens commissioned George Gibbs an ethnologist to survey the Puget Sound Indians and conduct a census. Gibbs found that the tribes had experienced a significant decline from an earlier census taken by the Hudson's Bay Company. Ibid., 25. Gibbs had been hired a few years earlier as an interpreter for the Northern California Indians, though he knew no Northern California tribes' languages, when Redick McKee, O. M. Wozencraft and George W. Barbour traveled through California making the "infamous" eighteen treaties in 1851-52. McKee was assigned the northern areas of California that Wozencraft was not visiting. Gibbs along with being an interpreter recorded his travels with McKee. He was also hired as an ethnologist on the Northern Transcontinental Railroad Survey and continued to work as one in Washington and Oregon territories. He drafted the treaties for the Native Americans in Willamette Valley and did the first comprehensive survey of Native Americans in the Puget Sound region.

Stevens' actions doomed the treaty process to end in failure. The differences between the white culture and the Native American culture were too great to be resolved quickly. The settlers' view of land ownership was the antithesis of the Native Americans' view. Whereas the Native Americans thought land was "owned" by the community each settler demanded "explicit title to the land."[77] Stevens was foolish to think he could bridge these differences in such a short amount of time.

Hostilities between the settlers and Native Americans began even before the last treaties were signed. Whether the treaties were directly responsible for the war is questionable.[78] But there is no question that the treaties hastened the war and created a "climate of distrust and hostility that made violence inevitable."[79]

The signing of the last treaty was on October 17, but the tensions were so high that a month before Native Americans killed three miners looking for gold on reservation land. A young Yakima warrior killed Andrew Bolton an Indian agent on the way to investigate the murders.[80] Trying to diffuse the situation, a large group of Yakimas met 102 soldiers sent to bring in the murderer. Before the Yakima chiefs could explain what had happened, someone fired shots. When it was over, five soldiers were dead and seventeen wounded. This battle marked the beginning of the Yakima War. The Native Americans spent the next four years (1855 to 1859) at war trying to save themselves from extermination.

An influential jurist in the Territory at the time, Judge Gilmore Hays, in an open letter published in the *Olympia, Washington Territory* September 12, 1856, stated that:

> Capt. McDonald . . . in charge of Fort Colville . . . told us that the Indians were dissatisfied with the sales they

[77]Dryden, *Dryden's History*, 125.

[78]"The immediate cause of Indian hostility lay in those treaties." Dryden, *Dryden's History*, 125. "What I [Gibbs] meant to show was that the war sprung partly from ill-judged legislation, partly from previously unratified treaties, and partly from recent blunders." A letter from Gibbs to Swan. Swan, *Northwest Coast*, 429.

[79]Buerge, "Isaac the Terrible," 27.

[80]Ironically, Agent Andrew J. Bolon's murder had nothing to do with either the treaties or the miners' death, but was the result of a young Yakima warrior seeking honors for killing an important white man. Glassley, *Indian Wars*, 111-113; Dryden, *Dryden's History*, 126.

had made of their lands, and that they were particularly hostile to Gov. Stevens and Gen. Palmer, who made the treaties. . . .

In the interview we held with Peu-pee-mox-mox, we found him in bad humor; he, too, was dissatisfied with the sales he had made of his lands; pretended as if he had not fully understood the bargains which he had made, and manifesting a strong dislike for Gov. Stevens. . . .

The immediate cause of the war grew out of the treaties, which had been made with the Indians for their lands. . . .[81]

There were of course a number of settlers who supported the war. "For ourselves, we know of but one course--but one feeling--and that is, as war exists, we are all for conquering a peace. If it be 'Governor Stevens' War,' we are all 'Gov. Stevens' men'."[82]

In 1886 Dr. Henry A. Smith wrote eleven reminiscences of the early pioneer days.[83] The ninth was a reminiscence of Stevens' days as governor and he wrote of Stevens:

Even those who believed the governor wrong never blamed him--for the sun itself has spots--and his many fine qualities of heart and head and his distinguished abilities manifested while acting as territorial governor and superintendent of Indian affairs, as well as upon the floors of congress [sic], made him almost a universal favorite and placed him high on the list of Washington Territory's many able governors and delegates.[84]

---

[81] *Olympia, Washington Territory,* 12 September 1856.

[82] *Pioneer and Democrat,* 26 October 1855, 1.

[83] Smith's 10th reminiscence was Seathl's speech.

[84] Clarence Bagley, *Bagley's Scrapbook,* No. 11 Special Collections, Washington University, Seattle, 19. The original was an article written in the *Seattle Times,* date unknown.

The flowery images common to his writings are not found in this reminiscence save for the metaphor of "sun spots."

One resident who defended Stevens wrote in the *Pioneer and Democrat*:

> We begin to think, out this way, that it is as much of a political war as it is a Injun-GUN-*powder* war. All the great guns of the teritory are mixt up in it - common guns - political guns - whig guns - aberlition guns – fuseion - *no nuthin GUNS* - and ev'n down to a little *pop-gunn* that belongs to the Puget Sound Cerrier. . . .
>
> People hear, have bin lookin round to see how Gov. Stevens has bin doin things since he got to this country, and a great many think he has dun rite smart for us; but most pursons think he has dun mity well indeed; I mean to say, the folks what live in the county and intends to stay hear for to live.[85]

Ezra Meeker was "a prominent pioneer"[86] and "known for marked individuality of character."[87] He was one of the strongest critics of Stevens' Indian policies and wrote, "the making of the Medicine Creek and Point Elliott Treaties was the sole cause of the war that followed."[88] Long after the events, a local newspaper wrote of him, "Meeker has the prestige of having been on the scene, and being personally in touch with the exciting events of fifty years ago . . ."[89]

Colonel Benjamin F. Shaw was the interpreter at both treaties and when asked if he could get the Indians to sign the Medicine Creek Treaty, he said:

---

[85]*Pioneer and Democrat*, 21 December 1855, 2. This author has reason to believe that the writer of this piece, Giles Scroggins, may be an alias for the editor or a literate citizen. "Scroggins" wrote at least one other letter in the *Pioneer and Democrat* defending Stevens and the misspellings appear too perfectly misspelled. It may have taken someone literate to have done such a good job spelling the words phonetically correct.

[86]Winther, *The Great Northwest*, 188.

[87]*The Oregonian*, Sunday April 2, 1905 in Clarence Bagley, *Bagley's Scrapbook*, No. 5 Special Collections, Washington University, Seattle, 80. Hereafter cited in the text as Bagley, *Scrapbook*, No. 5.

[88]Meeker, *Reminiscences*, 228.

[89]*The Patriarch*, 22 April 1905, 1.

Yes, I can get the Indians to sign their death warrant. Their [government officials] idea was in a few years the Indians would die out and the reservations would be large enough. My opinion is that the treaties were humbugs - premature, and the Indians did not understand them.[90]

Owen Bush, a pioneer on the Sound, was presented at both signings and he said he could speak the Indian languages,

But Stevens did not seem to want anyone to interpret in their own tongue, and had that done in Chinook. Of course, it was utterly impossible to explain the treaties to them in Chinook. Stevens wanted me to go to into war, but I wouldn't do it, I knew it was his bad management that brought on the war, and wouldn't raise a gun against those people who had always been so kind to us when we were so weak and needy.[91]

Ezra Meeker claimed Stevens was drunk at the council meetings, "intoxicated and unfit for transacting business while making these treaties."[92] George Gibbs was present at both treaty signings and acted as secretary at the Point Elliott Treaty.[93] He wrote a letter to the Secretary of State saying, Stevens "has been further inflamed by immoderate use of ardent spirits, and in his fits of intoxication knows

---

[90]Brackets are Ezra Meekers. Quoted in Meeker's *Reminiscences* from a paper read before the Washington Historical Society by Hon. James Wickersham, "The Indian Side of the Puget Sound War," Meeker, *Reminiscences*, 250-1.
[91]Ibid, 20.
[92]Ibid., 258. This accusation was strongly contested by Professor Edmond S. Meany, professor at the Washington State University, an authority of Northwest history and a great admirer of Stevens. "[Meany is] Completely and sentimentally devoted to the region, Meany's countless articles and books bore the unmistakable stamp of the frontier historian and romanticizer of the 'heroic past." Warren, *Farthest Frontier*, 277; Edmond Meany could step aside from his scrupulous and sagacious scholarship in his *History of the State of Washington* to add. . . press-agent boosting for the state" Cantwell, *Hidden Northwest*, 249.
[93]Meeker, *Reminiscences*, 263.

no bounds to his language or his actions."[94] In the *Washington Republican* June 5, 1857, "We have a right to resent public officials exhibiting themselves drunk. . . . he appears intoxicated on important public occasions . . ."[95] Gibb's interest in linguistics evolved into writing dictionaries of several native tongues in the area. Even the *Pioneer and Democrat*, a Democratic mouthpiece for Stevens,[96] begrudgingly wrote that Gibbs was "learned [enough] in the Indian vocabulary and tongue, to competently perform his duty . . ."[97] James Swan, who was present for the treaty on the Chehalis River, witnessed the exact opposite behavior from Stevens. He said when a Chief came drunk Stevens became "very much incensed at this breach of his orders, for he had expressly forbidden either whites or Indians bringing one drop of liquor into camp."[98] Swan went on to say that during the treaty on the Chehalis River Stevens spent four days during the treaty proceedings giving the Indians the evenings to discuss the day's proceedings. "Throughout the whole of the conference Governor Stevens evinced a

---

[94] *Pioneer and Democrat*, 10 April 1857, 1.

[95] Quoted in Meeker, *Reminiscences*, 258-9. When Meeker first published his book *Pioneer Reminscences* in 1905 it created quite a furor created. Professor Edmond S. Meany, professor at the Washington State University, an authority of Northwest history and a great admirer of Stevens, wrote a series of blistering attacks in the *Seattle Daily Times* and the *Washington Republican* against Meeker's treatment of Stevens, Stevens' alleged intoxication, and blaming Stevens for the Indian wars. Bagley, *Scrapbook*, No. 5; *Seattle Daily Times*, 15 April; 1, 5 May 1905. *Washington Republican*, 5 June 1857, 2.

[96] ". . . he strengthened his Democratic political base by transforming the only newspaper, the *Washington Pioneer* into a Democratic mouthpiece, renamed the Washington *Pioneer and Democrat* in February 1854." Buerge, "Isaac the Terrible," 28. "*The Columbian*, the first newspaper in the region north of the Columbia River, which was launched in 1852, also started as a 'neutral in politics,' according to its owners. A year later it was sold, and the new editor changed its name to *Pioneer and Democrat*." Warren, *Farthest Frontier*, 193.

[97] *Washington Republican*, 5 June 1857, p. 2. "in 1857, the plant of the defunct *Courier* was utilized to turn out a campaign sheet called the *Washington Republican*. It was founded solely to promote the election of a party candidate to Congress and endured only as long as the campaign issue." Warren, *Farthest Frontier*, 193.

[98] Swan, *Northwest Coast*, 347. Shaw was the chief interpreter, Simmons was one of the Indian agents and Gibbs was the secretary to the commission during the treaty on the Chehalis River.

degree of forbearance, and a desire to do every thing [*sic*] he could for the benefit of the Indians. Nothing was done in a hurry."[99]

But if any of these charges against Stevens were true, it might not be surprising that Stevens misread the Indians' intentions and thought they looked forward to their "speedy extinction."[100] For Stevens to use only Chinook jargon to explain the treaties was a calculating move on his part because as Owen Bush said "it was utterly impossible to explain the treaties to them in Chinook."[101] So when it came time for Seathl to sign a treaty it was impossible for him to know exactly what he was signing; furthermore, Seathl refused to speak Chinook jargon. On that fateful day in January when the two met, Seathl inevitably spoke in his native tongue when he gave the speech to Governor Stevens. The interpreters translated the speech into Chinook jargon and then into English. Translations by their nature lose something in the transition from one language to another. If the rich language of Seathl's people was reduced to a language of five hundred words and then translated again into the English language much would be lost.[102] If it was impossible to explain treaties using this process, it is questionable how accurately interpreters could translate Seathl's words from Chinook jargon into English or for that matter, how accurately his words could have been translated into Chinook jargon. Swan also noted the difficulty in translating treaty terms with Chinook jargon.

The Point Elliott Treaty of 1855, which Seathl signed and the Senate failed to ratify, left the Indians impoverished within three years

---

[99]Swan, *Northwest Coast*, 348. "I think Governor Stevens's course admirably adapted to conciliate the Indians, and although I have asserted that he erred in judgment in wishing to place the five tribes on one reservation, yet his whole thought and object was for their good, and there can be no doubt that, had they acceded to his views, they would have benefited." Ibid., 351.

[100]In a biography of Stevens, Richard Kent wrote of Stevens' attitude towards the Native Americans that "Above all, he had great confidence in his own ability to handle the Indians. This cocksureness had developed as he came west with the railroad survey; he had expected the worst, particularly from the Blackfeet, but the survey party had come through with no serious incidents. Stevens did not recognize that their good fortune resulted in large measure from the excellent liaison work of Alexander Culbertson. Stevens exaggerated his own role and assumed that the other whites either had not known how to handle the Indians successfully, or had overestimated the danger." Kent, *Stevens*, 194.

[101]Meeker, *Reminiscences*, 208.

[102]A trade language of five hundred words, which was a mixture of English and the local native languages. It was used among the Northwest Indians and whites.

of its signing. During this time, while war raged around him, "Seathl remained doggedly faithful to the settlers at Elliott Bay [Seattle]. . . . "[103] and managed to keep his people free from involvement in the war. "Now Leschi and his people went toward Seattle, to White river, and all over where there were white settlements, killing and killing. Leschi got to Seattle and old s'iy'a`l [Seathl] came to him and said, 'No, Leschi, don't kill these white people. Yesler and others of them have Indian women. Don't kill them. Take my word.' Well, Leschi said to s'iy'a`l, 'All right, we'll take your word. We won't kill them.'"[104] Seathl also warned the local white populations when hostile Indian attacks were imminent. In 1870 one of the local newspapers wrote "This good old chief was always a friend to the whites; and throughout the last Indian war in the Territory he remained at home, taking no part in the contest."[105] Is the man who emerges from Dr. Smith's transcription "a good old chief" and "a friend to the whites" or a "defiant angry man" as noted by a staff member of the National Archives Jerry L. Clark. Clark wrote an article for the *Journal of the National Archives* on the history of Seathl and his speech. In the 1985 article Clark wrote that the National Archives had found "the historical record suggests that the compliant and passive individual named Seattle is not recognizable in the image of the defiant angry man whose words reverberate in our time."[106] Are the words and sentences found in a few sections of the speech Smith transcribed reflective of Seathl's hostility and harsh criticism of the whites, as Clark seemed to believe? Seathl's disposition towards the whites is not easy to glean from this speech. His actions during the war obviously speak of his friendship, but there are sections in the speech that seemed to contradict this friendliness:

> He [the white man's God] gave the white man laws but
> He had no word for His red children whose teeming
> millions filled this vast continent as the stars fill the

[103]Winther, *The Great Northwest*, 175.

[104]From an interview in 1940 with Frank Allen, a Skokomish Indian by William W. Elmendorf. William W. Elmendorf, *Twana Narratives* 154 (38.2).

[105]*Weekly Intelligencer* (Seattle), 25 April 1870, 1. "When the first settlers came to the Sound, Seattle let it be known that he was their friend and there are none of the early pioneers but who attest to his friendship for the whites." Bagley, *History of Seattle*, 78.

[106]Jerry Clark, "Thus Spoke Chief Seattle: The Story of an Undocumented Speech" *Journal of the National Archives* vol. 17 No. 1 (Spring 1985), 64. Hereafter cited in the text as Clark, "Thus Spoke."

firmament. No, we are two distinct races and must ever remain so. There is little in common between us. . . .

The white man's God cannot love his red children or he would protect them. They seem to be orphans and can look nowhere for help. How can we become brothers? How can your father become our father and bring us prosperity and awaken in us dreams of returning greatness?

The Indian's night promises to be dark. No bright star hovers about the horizon . . .

The very dust under your feet responds more lovingly to our footsteps than to yours.[107]

To consider these passages expressions of hostility and harsh criticism may very well be a Eurocentric analysis of Seathl's message. Professor Albert Wahrhaftig of Sonoma State University has pointed out that these sentiments were common among Native Americans at the time and that invariably they held themselves accountable for the fate that had befallen them because of their own failure to live according to the traditions and customs of their ancestors. The feeling that they "have been abandoned and neglected; whites are better off; the future looks dim" are more "explanations of their predicament . . ., but [are] not . . . expressions of outrage against a more favored white man."[108] As a young man, according to Hudson's' Bay Company officials, Seathl was a "bellicose war leader character" and they banned him from the post for a time. But by the time the Americans were arriving in the 1850s the settlers who lived there knew Seathl more for his friendliness than any hostility. This may have more to do with his "emergence as an elder that required diplomacy and tact."[109]

[107]Smith, *Seattle Star*, 7.
[108]Albert Wahrhaftig, Sebastopol, California to Daniel Markwyn, Rohnert Park, California, 1 April 1997, wahrhaft@metro.net To daniel.markwyn@SONOMA.EDU.
[109]Buerge, "We Call Seattle," 24.

The last actor in this play of events was a twenty-two-year-old man who arrived in Seattle late in 1852, Dr. Henry Allen Smith.[110] Smith was living in Keokuk, Iowa when Dr. Jay Millard, a relative who was organizing a wagon train, offered him a place on the wagon train if he would act as its doctor, and he could join for two hundred dollars. By the time the wagons left, his mother and sister had joined him. They arrived in Portland in late October. Smith heard that Stevens was surveying a route for the northern railroad. Responding to the lure of wealth, he joined the many people moving to Puget Sound. San Francisco had become the main Pacific port and the biggest city in the West. The city that connected the two coasts by railroad was the city destined to be the wealthiest in the West. Smith gambled the location of the Pacific terminus would be in Puget Sound. In November he headed to Olympia, Washington. Here he met a "rough-looking, heavy-set man, whose whole personality denoted energy and courage" by the name of Luther Collins. Luther told Smith in "three days time I will land you in the Garden of Eden"--the future site of Seattle.[111] He met Dr. Maynard on this trip. It was in front of Dr. Maynard's store that Chief Seathl stood before Governor Stevens and spoke the words that Smith published thirty-three years later in a local newspaper.[112]

Smith acquired one hundred and sixty acres on one of the bays near Dr. Maynard's and by 1853 built his first log cabin. A year later he added an infirmary. He also started the first grafted orchard in Washington Territory that year. "Like many of his contemporaries, he was fascinated by the Indians. He quickly picked up enough Chinook jargon . . . to manage them as laborers, but he also inquired about their

---

[110]He was born on April 11, 1830 in Wooster, Ohio. Bagley, *History of Seattle*, Clarence Bagley, *History of Seattle: A Volume of Memoires and Genealogy of Representative Citizen of the City of Seattle and County of King Washington Including Biographies of Many of Those Who Have Past Away* (New York: Lewis Publishing Co., 1903). Herbert Hunt, *Historical and Description: The Indian, Pioneer, The Modern*, (Chicago: S.J. Clarke Co., 1917), 264. Hereafter cited in the text as Bagley, *Volume of Memories*.

[111]Dr. Henry A. Smith, account of his journey quoted in C.T. Conover, "Just Cogitating: Dr. Henry A. Smith Tells of Early Sound Life," *Seattle Sunday Times*, 17 August 1958, 8; David M. Buerge, "The Man Who Invented Chief Seattle," *Seattle Weekly*, 1 September 1993, 20. Hereafter cited in the text as Buerge, "Man Who Invented."

[112]Stevens wrote that his purpose was "to visit and take a census of the Indian tribes, learn something of the general character of the Sound and its harbors." Stevens, *Life of Stevens*, 1:416-7.

lives."[113] The local newspapers often printed basic Chinook jargon vocabulary[114] "for the benefit of new comers into this Territory."[115]

Smith took an active interest in the local Indians, learning their folklore and for a time serving as the physician on the Tulalip reservation in Snohomish County. "He wrote for the press and for the magazines, and especially for the Indians and the character of Chief Seattle, of whom he was a great admirer."[116] The *Weekly-Intelligencer* in 1873 carried an article he wrote titled "Our Aborigines: Their Destiny - Reservation, Schools, Etc., Etc." A few fragments of the article give an indication of the words and style he used in Seathl's speech and his sympathy for the Native Americans.

> May it be pardonable in us for pausing a moment for the purpose of gleaning a few facts in relation to that people in our midst, now so rapidly passing away. Their former status is but dimly lymned [illegible] in the swiftly gathering shadows of spent day, whose deepening twilight will soon merge into a night so dark that the historian's pen alone, will be able to cast a single ray upon the voice-less gloom[117]

Note the Victorian fustian with its heavy use of metaphors in describing the plight of the local Native Americans:

> gathering shadows of spent day,
> deepening twilight

---

[113]Buerge, "Man Who Invented," 20.

[114]Vanderwerth, *Oratory*, 119. "Smith . . . mastered the Duwamish language in about two years." Ibid. "According to a number of local historians of Seattle, Dr. Smith was fluent in the Duwamish tongue and thus was able to transcribe Seattle's words verbatim." Clark, "Thus Spoke" 62. There is no evidence to believe Smith knew anything but Jargon.

[115]*Seattle Weekly*, 3 September 1864, 1. There is a list of Jargon words and their English equivalent in this issue of the *Seattle Weekly*. Buerge states "In 1853, *The Columbian*, the territorial's sole newspaper, had published lists of Jargon words and their translations." Buerge, "Seattle's King Arthur," 28. This author was unable to find these lists in *The Columbian* and further research is needed.

[116]C.T. Conover, *Seattle Sunday Times*, 22 August 1948, 4.

[117]Henry A. Smith, *Weekly-Intelligencer* 30 August 1873, 1.

merge into a night so dark that the historian's pen alone,
to cast a single ray upon the voice-less gloom

and compare it to the metaphors and similes found in Seathl's speech:

> . . . my people are ebbing away like a fast-receding tide,
> The Indian's night promises to be dark. . .
> Sad-voiced winds moan in the distance. . .
> . . . their deep fastnesses at eventide grow shadowy with the presence of dusky spirits.[118]

In 1863 Smith arrived in Snohomish County.[119] He left his farm in Seattle because the city's fortunes and future appeared to be waning and many people were moving away. In an attempt to entice people to settle Snohomish County, Smith wrote a series of articles in the local newspapers. In an early article he described the falls on the Snoqualmie River:

> This is truly a sublime spectacle, the river dashes over a perpendicular bank and is precipitated 300 feet into the boiling, foaming flood below; eternal rainbows circle round in gorgeous beauty, losing themselves ever and anon in snowy columns of spray that continually rise and ascend far over the gigantic pines above. . . . [120]

Compare the florid use of description here with Seathl's words as he describes his people:

> our people covered the whole land, as the waves of a wind-ruffled sea cover its shell-paved floor.

In another article he describes the possible gold fields on the Skykomish River: "Who knows but in the old and dusty beds thousands of fortunes await the magic touch of miners' wand to hasten the 'glorious sun-burst of a brighter day' soon to dawn upon our

[118]Smith, *Seattle Star*, 7.
[119]Snohomish County is less than thirty miles north of Seattle.
[120]Buerge, "Man Who Invented," 22.

Territory."[121] In 1871 he wrote three articles describing the Snohomish and Stillaguuamish Rivers in the *Weekly-Intelligencer*. For the most part his prose was straightforward: "The valley here, and for a distance of five or six miles wide is excellent soil, formed by alluvial deposits, but it all overflows during freshlets." In only one does he write briefly in fustian:

> Here will sometime, and that time is not very future, be
> the paradise of husbandman
> When golden harvests to the scythe will bend
> And prove the forests' terrors at an end;
> And happy children thronging home from school
> Give earnest of refinement's coming rule.[122]

These quotations show a writer quite capable of writing in the florid Victorian style found in the speech. People in the Puget Sound region knew him as a "poet of no ordinary talent" who "wove into verse and essays much of his musings."[123] His daughter, Mrs. Ione Smith Graff, wrote a memoir of her father, and said "When Papa died in 1915 at the age of 85, he left six ledger-size volumes of poems written in longhand. A few were published under the pen name Paul Garland, by *Sunset Magazine*."[124] It is important to consider Smith's ability as a poet, writer and his knowledge of local Native American folklore when studying his transcription of the speech. The speech has images and concepts that only a Native American or one versed in the folklore could know. His article entitled "Aborigines" show this knowledge. The question remains, what did Seathl speak and what did Smith create? Seathl never learned English so the florid Victorian prose found in the speech is not his.[125] Another consideration is that there

---

[121]Ibid., 21.

[122]Henry A. Smith, *Weekly-Intelligencer*, 27 March 1871, 2.

[123]Frederic James Grant, *History of Seattle* (New York: American Publishing Co. 1891), 432. Hereafter cited in the text as Grant, *History*.

[124]Ione Smith Graff, "Memoirs of Dr. Henry A. Smith," 1957, 6, Transcript at the Museum of History and Industry, Seattle, Washington. No one has found these ledgers. *Sunset Magazine* has no record of any published pieces by Paul Garland; there were, however, other magazines during this time called *Sunset*. David Buerge, interview by the author, 12 March 1995, Seattle, Washington, telephone.

[125]For a more detailed discussion of oral traditions see Appendix 14.

are other examples of Smith's writings that are quite similar to the speech.

His articles describing the "aborigines" and Snohomish County are some of the earliest writings found that bear his signature and are similar in style to Seathl's speech. They are all heavily laden with metaphors and similes. There is, however, an article in an 1853 issue of the *Columbian* that an anonymous author wrote entitled, "The Immortal Dead" that has a similar ring in content to later words Smith would write. "How unchanging is their love for us. How tenderly they look down upon us and how closely they surround."[126] Only months later, Seathl is quoted by Smith saying "they ever yearn in tenderest affection over the lonely hearted living and often return to visit and comfort them."[127] The similarities are too great to consider this a coincidence.

The only indication that his transcription is accurate is Dr. Smith's word and the oral tradition of the Suquamish Nation.[128] There is, however, documentation of the meeting. The paths of Chief Seathl, Governor Isaac I. Stevens and Dr. Henry A. Smith crossed in January 1854 in front of Dr. Maynard's store in the town of Seattle. With them were 120 white residents and almost 1200 of Seathl's people.[129] These three men were there for different reasons and sought different goals, but the forces that brought them together were identical. It was Dr. Smith's ambition that led him halfway across the continent to begin a new life. His ambition was similar to that of many emigrants: to find his fortune in this new land. Governor Stevens' ambition to "gain for himself in a year [in Washington Territory] what it might take decades or lifetimes to accomplish in the East."[130] The resettlement of Chief Seathl and his people was a small problem compared to the larger challenge of establishing a territorial government. Chief Seathl on the other hand was facing the possible extinction of his people and at least the loss of his homeland. For him, Stevens' "small problem" was no less than the survival of his people.

The successful westward expansion of the United States territory laid the foundation upon which their paths would cross. The land gained from Mexico by conquest and from Great Britain by treaty

---

[126]Buerge, "Seattle's King Arthur," 28.

[127]Smith, *Seattle Star*, 7.

[128] Jones, 14 September 2007.

[129]Buerge, "Seattle's King Arthur," 28.

[130]Buerge, "Isaac the Terrible," 25.

gave Americans the entire western end of the continent between the 49th parallel and 33rd parallel and three years later the wealth from the California Gold Rush. With the wave of gold seekers came markets for the products of Oregon and Washington that allowed for the continual growth of these territories. One minor incident in the drama of the settling of the Far West was the meeting of these three men. Smith turned this meeting from an obscure diplomatic discourse into a piece of inspirational local Puget Sound history. Whether Smith's words reflected the thoughts of Seathl remains uncertain. Without Smith's notes of that meeting there is no documentation to corroborate Smith's version of the speech. There is, however, verification that Stevens and Seathl were there on January 12, 1854, and excellent circumstantial evidence that Smith was present when Stevens and Seathl spoke to each other.

The setting for Seathl's speech appears to have been a visit made by Governor Stevens in January 1854 to the town of Seattle. On January 11, 1854, *The Pioneer,* a local newspaper, noted that the "Governor took his departure for a trip down the Sound on Monday last . . . We understand the object of his tour is to institute an investigation into the condition of Indian affairs in that direction . . ."[131] Stevens wrote that his purpose was:

> to visit and take as census of the Indian tribes, learn something of the general character of the Sound and its harbors . . .

> In this trip I visited Steilacoom, Seattle . . . We examined the coalmines back of Seattle and Bellingham Bay, and saw a large body of Indians of nearly all tribes. I was greatly impressed with the importance of Seattle . . .[132]

[131] *The Pioneer,* 11 January 1854.

[132] Stevens, *Life of Stevens,* 416-7. The following was part of the quote: "Skagit Head, Penn's Cove, the mouths of the Skagit and Samish rivers, Bellingham Bay, passed up the channel De Rosario and down the channel De Haro to Victoria, and on my return made Port Townsend and several other points on the western shore of the Sound." Ibid.; "I was greatly impressed with Elliott's Bay, on which are the flourishing towns of Seattle and Alki . . ." A report to the Secretary of War, quoted in Stevens, *Life of Stevens,* 417.

In 1855 at the Point Elliott Treaty proceedings Stevens spoke to the council of chiefs recalling when he had been there a year earlier and spoken with them:

> Did I not come through your country one year since? . . . I came through your country . . . to know what you were, to know what you wanted, to know your grievances,[133]

David Buerge has placed the date of the meeting between Seathl and Stevens as January 12.

> [the speech] was delivered in his [Seathl's] native tongue and translated into . . . Chinook Jargon by an Indian interpreter. This may in turn, have been translated into English by George Gibbs, Stevens' assistant, who had translated the governor's remarks into Jargon for the benefit of the Indians.[134]

Some people think Seathl gave the speech at the signing of the Point Elliott Treaty, which took place in January of 1855.[135] The treaty proceedings are on record and the speech that Smith took notes of and later transcribed was not given then. Others have claimed the "speech" was a letter to President Franklin Pierce in 1854 or 1855.[136] Still others

---

[133]Stevens, *Life of Stevens*, 464.

[134]Buerge, "Seattle's King Arthur," 28; Stevens, *Life of Stevens*, 463. Buerge did not cite his source.

[135]William Arrowsmith, "Speech of Chief Seattle", *Arion*, 8:461-464, 1969, 461; "Chief Seattle . . . delivered a prophetic speech, in 1854, to mark the transferal of ancestral Indian lands to the federal government." "The Decidedly Unforked Message Of Chief Seattle," Northwest Airline Magazine *Passages*, April, 1974, 19; Frederick J. Dockstader, *Great North American Indians Profiles in Life and Leadership* (San Francisco: Van Nostrand Reinhold Co., 1977), 258.

[136]Campbell, *Power of Myth*, 33-5; "The following letter, written in 1855, was sent to President Franklin Pierce by Chief Sealth. . . This letter was reprinted in the October 1973 newsletter published by the Environmental Education Council of Milwaukee" *Exclusively Yours*, Vol. 27, Issue 4, April 1974, (Milwaukee: Patten Co. Inc.) 31; "A Letter From Chief Seattle" *Outdoor America*, December 1975) 6; "For Your Children," *Wildlife Omnibus*, 15 November 1973, 30; "This earth is sacred," *Environmental Action*, 11 November 1972, 7.

have said Seathl gave the speech in December 1854,[137] but Smith's introduction to the speech clearly contradicts these dates:

> When Governor Stevens first arrived in Seattle and told the natives he had been appointed commissioner of Indian affairs for Washington Territory, they gave him a demonstrative reception . . . Placing one hand on the governor's head . . . he [Seathl] commenced his memorable speech. . . .[138]

If this was the case, then the speech could not have been given at the treaty signing or in December of 1854. The date would have to be the fall or winter 1853-1854, the year he became governor. President Pierce appointed Stevens governor earlier in the year and Stevens was in command of the Northern Railroad Survey. So he did not arrive in the capital of Washington Territory, Olympia, until November 25, 1853. He did take a trip to Washington on March 26, 1854, and returned on December 7, 1854. This may have led to the mistaken belief that "first arrived" referred to his return from this trip, which would have given credence to the belief it was in December of 1854.[139] But Stevens' January tour of 1854 seems to be the most likely date. He came by boat and arrived on the 10th. The next day he visited a mine on the Duwamish River and on the 12th spoke with Seathl.[140]

In any case, there is no record of a letter from Seathl in either the private papers of President Pierce in the New Hampshire Historical Society or the Presidential Papers of Pierce in the Library of Congress.[141] The staff at the National Archives has been unable to

---

[137]Museum of History and Industry, *The Famous of Chief Seattle,* (Seattle: Museum of History and Industry), 1; John Rich,"Seattle's Unanswered Challenge," (Fairfield, Washington: Ye Galleon Press. 1932/1970), 27. Hereafter cited in the text as Rich, *Challenge.*"The Famous Oration of Chief Seattle," (Seattle: Museum of History and Industry, 1990), 1.

[138]Smith, *Seattle Star,* 7.

[139]Stevens, *Life of Stevens,* 414, 425.

[140]Buerge, "Seattle's King Arthur," 28.

[141]Clark, "Thus Spoke", 61. John C. Broderick of the Manuscript Division of the Library of Congress 1 April 1977 in reply to an inquiry by Lennart Norl`en at the Institute Forestal Latinoamericano in Venezuela about the authenticity of the "letter." 20 March 1977, Transcript at The Seattle Museum of History and Industry, Seattle, Washington. In a letter to Janice Krenmayr, Richard S. Maxwell of Natural Resources

locate any "letter" among the records of the Bureau of Indian Affairs in the National Archives and "concluded that the letter . . . is probably spurious."[142]

It would be quite improbable if not impossible for a letter from the Chief of the Suquamish to the President of the United States not to have been recorded in at least one of the governmental offices through which it passed. For the letter to have made it to the desk of the President it would have passed through at least six departments: the local Indian agent, Colonel Simmons; to the superintendent of Indian Affairs, Gov. Stevens; to the Commissioner of Indian Affairs; to the office of the Secretary of the Interior and finally to the President's desk--quite a paper trail for the letter to have left not a trace. It can be concluded that no letter was written for Seathl[143] and sent to President Pierce or to any other President.

There is no documentation to support Smith's statement that he witnessed a meeting between Governor Stevens and Chief Seathl, but it is safe to assume he was there. Since it was hard to travel between settlements, no resident would miss the first visit of the first governor of Washington Territory. There is also no documentation that Stevens and Seathl met or the date of that supposed meeting. But

---

Branch of the Civil Archives Division of the National Archives and Records Service, wrote that there was no letter from Seattle to Pierce in the Bureau of Indian Affairs and gave her the addresses of the New Hampshire Historical Society, Manuscript Division of the Library of Congress and Bowdoin College all of which she checked and they had no record of the letter. Richard S. Maxwell, Washington D.C., to Janice Krenmayr, Seattle, 18 September 1974, Transcript at The Seattle Museum of History and Industry, Seattle, Washington.

[142]Crawford wrote that "our staff has spent considerable time and effort attempting to locate the letter or find some indication that Seattle did write the letter, but have been unable to do so." Richard C. Crawford of the Natural Resources Branch Civil Archives Division, 6 April 1977, to Lennart Norlen in response to Norlen's inquiry as to the authenticity of the "letter," Richard C. Crawford, Washington D.C., to Lennart Norlen, Seattle, Washington, 6 April 1977. Transcript at The Seattle Museum of History and Industry, Seattle, Washington. Crawford, Richard C., Washington D.C., to Jodi Perlman-Cohen, Littleton, Colorado, 17 August 1976. Hereafter cited in the text as Crawford, *Letter to Norlen*. Richard C. Crawford of the Natural Resources Branch of the Civil Archives Division of the National Archives and Records Service, 2 November 1976, to E. Nolan of the Seattle Historical Society in response to Nolan's inquiry as to the authenticity of the "letter," Richard C. Crawford, Washington D.C., to E. Nolan, Seattle, Washington, 2 November 1976. Transcript at The Museum of History and Industry, Seattle, Washington.

[143]Since Seathl did not speak English he obviously could not write English.

the local newspaper published Stevens' itinerary that included a stop in Seattle and Stevens mentions this visit a year later during the Point Elliott Treaty proceedings. His own writing clearly shows when he made the trip, the reasons for the trip and that he met with the local Indians. So it can be safely assumed that the most important Native American among the surrounding tribes, Seathl, was there to greet the first governor of the territory of Washington. But again the problem arises as to the authenticity of Smith's version of Seathl's speech that day.

Smith is the only one who claimed to take notes during the meeting or to document what transpired. There are, however, government documents with speeches given by Seathl on other occasions that government officials duly recorded at the time: the Point Elliott Treaty and the plea to the Indian Agent, Michael Simmons, for example. There is also another speech recorded by Benjamin Shaw. These records are all the written evidence available to compare Smith's transcription and validate his version.

Another question that arises over Smith's publication of the speech is why the thirty-three year delay? The meeting between Governor Stevens and Chief Seathl took place on January 12, 1854. The first time anyone presented the speech to the public was in the October 29, 1887, edition of *Seattle Sunday Star*. Smith wrote eleven reminiscences of Puget Sound's early pioneer days and Seathl's speech was the tenth in the series. The reason for the delay may lie in the political and economic climate of 1887.

Chapter III

The Mystery of the Thirty-three Year Lapse[144]

Smith published his version of Seathl's speech as the Puget Sound began to emerge from the grip of a depression. The Sound had just been through a tumultuous period with anti-Chinese riots throughout the region and the rise to power of the People's Party. George Kinnear was a captain of the local militia and wrote of these times that:

> A general unrest existed all over the country, business was depressed, times were stringent, men were out of employment, the usual distress that goes with such periods prevailed, making it easy for designing men to organize discontented forces to attack some real or imaginary causes of their troubles, and in this section of the country where there were many Chinese employed, it was believed that if the Mongolians could be driven

---

[144] In the late 1960's, Dr. William Arrowsmith, a professor in Classical Studies, translated the speech from the Victorian prose of Smith's to a closer rendition of how Seathl may have spoken (for a more detailed discussion of this matter see Appendix 6). Arrowsmith said "It was obvious that Smith was trying to make the best possible case for a people who had no voice." Professor William Arrowsmith, interviewed by the author, 29 October 1991, Sebastopol, California, telephone. Hereafter cited in the text as Arrowsmith, 29 October. "Later, when it became bleakly clear that Seattle's people were being threatened with extinction, Smith 'worked up' the speech, expanding . . . and embellishing it thickly . . . What better way to arouse a sense of conscience in the white man than to have an Indian speak to him in terms of his own classic texts and the values implicit in those texts." William Arrowsmith, Boston, Massuchusetts, to Daniel Miller, Aptos, California, 26 November 1989, Daniel Miller, Aptos California. Hereafter cited in the text as Arrowsmith to Miller 26 November 1989. For the complete text of the letter see Appendix 15.

out of the country, more employment would be given to the white labor.[145]

Smith's decision to publish the speech may have been in response to this political and economic maelstrom.

According to David Buerge who has been researching the lives of Smith, Seathl and the speech for over thirty years,[146] Smith wrote the speech in response to the political power struggle between Seattle's original pioneers, and those who came in the 1870s and 80s. The pioneers were "middle-class landowners, a propertied elite that liked to call itself 'Old Seattle.'"[147] In reaction to them, the newcomers "styled themselves as 'New Seattle.'" Their ranks included an unlikely group of "growing working class and a class of urban professionals and entrepreneurs."[148] 'New Seattle's' opposition to 'Old Seattle' was one of the few issues that united the working class, the urban professionals and the entrepreneurs.

In the early 1880s tensions began building between pioneers and the newcomers. But the depression of 1884 and the subsequent anti-Chinese riots intensified those tensions and drew the line between the working-class citizens of Seattle and "Old Seattle" and turned the issues into a conflict of classes. In the election of 1886, the early pioneers lost their decades-old political control. This shift in power was the direct result of the bitter hostility that surrounded the Chinese issue coupled with the Depression.

> The Seattle violence [towards the Chinese] illustrates the economic difficulties of the period, the class cleavages, and the specific grievances against the Chinese which are to be found in other outbursts [of

---

[145] George Kinnear, *Anti-Chinese Riots At Seattle, Wn., February 8th, 1886* (Seattle, Washington: Twenty-fifth Anniversary of Riots, February 8th, 1911), 3. Hereafter cited in the text as Kinnear, *Anti-Chinese Riots.*

[146] David Buerge is writing a book soon to be published on the relationship between Chief Seathl and Smith and how each of their lives and personalities affected the speech.

[147] Smith was an original pioneer and lifelong Republican whose sympathies lay with "Old Seattle," although he doctored and was friend to the laboring man.

[148] Buerge, "Seattle's King Arthur," 28.

violence against the Chinese throughout the Far West].[149]

The Depression, the anti-Chinese sentiment and the election of 1886 may have ultimately influenced Smith to publish the speech thirty-three years after it was spoken. Each of these factors played a role in deepening the schism that developed between the original pioneers and the new emigrants.

We must consider the role-played by the Chinese in the economics of the Far West if we are to understand how the Depression and the anti-Chinese sentiment dovetailed, creating the political turmoil that tore through the Pacific Northwest. Chinese laborers had been an issue in the territorial politics of Washington and Oregon as well as California for some time. The issue of the Chinese in Washington State was "minor in 1880 and a dominant one in 1886. . . . When times were good, the presence of gangs of Chinese labor indicated large construction work. . ."[150] The depression that descended upon the Pacific Northwest in 1884 exacerbated the situation.[151] With massive

---

[149] Jules Alexander Karlin, "The Anti-Chinese Outbreaks in Seattle, 1885-1886" (reprint, *The Pacific Northwest Quarterly*, Vol. 39, No. 2, Seattle, Washington, April, 1948), quoted in Roger Daniels, ed., *Anti-Chinese Violence in North America*, (New York: Arno Press, 1978), 103. Hereafter cited in the text as Daniels, *Anti-Chinese Violence*.

[150] Robert C. Nesbit, *"He Built Seattle:" A Biography of Judge Thomas Burke*, (Seattle: University of Washington Press, 1961) 61. Hereafter cited in the text Nesbit, *Judge Burke*. "An editor in Olympia watched a Chinese gardener raking maple leaves of his prosperous employer . . . ." and wrote "urging the farmers to take a lesson in thrift and agriculture." David Edward Wynne, "Reaction to the Chinese in the Pacific Northwest and British Columbia 1850 to 1910" (Ph.D. diss, University of Washington, 1964; reprint, New York: Arno Press, New York Times Co., 1978), iv. Hereafter cited in the text as Wynne, *Reaction to the Chinese*.

[151] California was the first of the Far Western territories to display this anti-Chinese sentiment with the Foreign Miners License Tax levied in 1850. In the same year the Oregon Territory census recorded just two Chinese. Twenty years later there were still only 234 Chinese in the Washington territory [Wynne, *Reaction to the Chinese*, 41]. The early Chinese migration into the Pacific Northwest in the 1860s was primarily Chinese trying their luck in the gold fields. By the 1860s and 1870s, Chinese were following on the heels of the white miners as the goldfields of Southwestern Oregon opened up, followed by more goldfields along the Snake River, the Clearwater and Upper Columbia rivers. When mining began to wane the Chinese picked hops, worked in the coal mines, fishing canneries, laundries and at other menial tasks [Avery, *History and Government*, 197]. The Chinese ran into continual opposition from the white miners and loggers, but were welcomed by the railroads the Northern

unemployment, Chinese and whites competed for what few jobs were available. Employers strapped for cash found it far more economical to hire the Chinese rather than the whites.[152]

The Depression turned the municipal election of 1884 into a bitter contest. The Business Man's Ticket, representing the conservative pioneers, wanted "business as usual." Their opponents, the People's Ticket, demanded reform because to them "the older values . . . of early . . . Washington founders . . . [had become] less and less appropriate to the new urban and industrial society."[153]

Within this political and economic context, tensions exploded in 1885 and began the deep divisions that formed in Seattle's political landscape. These divisions and the hostility that was eventually directed towards the original pioneers, "the wagon-train aristocracy,"[154] had a

---

Pacific and Canadian Pacific. In 1877 the Messrs. Tull & Co., a fishing cannery, laid off all their Chinese workers and hired whites. *The Northern Star* applauded this decision writing, "There is one firm operating our fisheries for the benefit of our country instead of the Mongolian Empire." *The Northern Star*, Seattle, 6 October 1877. Yet, when the same paper reported on the railroad construction that was bringing the railroads to Olympia the article was "on the exclusive use of Chinese labor. . . without adverse comments." Ibid., 24 April 1878. All of the following was quoted in Wynne, *Reaction to the Chinese*, 81. The railroads imported shiploads of Chinese to the Puget Sound during their construction.

[152]The living and working conditions in China were responsible for making the Chinese so economical to hire, "that these Chinese would be at once important productive units and serious competitors is indicated by their low standard of living and their industrious habits. The Chinese peasant and farm laborer is accustomed to the hardest kind of work and the most careful avoidance of all waste. . . In the absence of organized immigrant labor, with unequal bargaining power, and with ignorance of the local market, these habits spell intensive competition and undercutting of native labor, if the two groups are engaged in the same occupation." Quoted by Rose Hum Lee, *The Chinese in the U.S.A.*, Hong Kong, 1960, 13, quoted in Wynne, *Reaction to the Chinese*, 40. A correspondent from *Harper's Magazine* traveled through the Puget Sound in 1884 and noted that "the unreliability of white labor 'which is fatal to success in many commercial ventures,' was the reason 'that the Chinese have been encouraged by capitalists.'" Ernest Ingersoll, 'From the Fraser to the Columbia,' *Harper's*, LXVII (April-May, 1884), 871, 876, quoted in Nesbit, *Judge Burke*, 170. Winther, *The Great Northwest*, 421.

[153]Robert L. Tyler, *Rebels of the Woods: the I.W.W. in the Pacific Northwest* (Eugene, Oregon: University of Oregon Books, 1967), 2. Hereafter cited in the text as Tyler, *Rebels of the Woods*.

[154]Ibid. Various groups who were Sino phobic called the original pioneers or "Old Seattle" a number of degrading names. The following names will be used in the text: dog-salmon aristocracy, old mossbacks and wagon-train aristocracy.

profound impact. Three pioneers began writing their memoirs and history of the first days of Seattle. At this time Arthur A. Denny, one of Seattle's founders, wrote of "people here now who have no good word for the old settler. . . These [people], however are degenerate scrubs."[155] Dr. Smith was one of these three pioneers writing memoirs. Rather than publish his memoirs, he wrote twelve reminiscences of the early days of Seattle in the local newspaper. His eleventh reminiscence was Seathl's speech. It laments the passing of one tribe as another tribe, the Americans, takes control. "They [the Americans] are like the grass that covers the vast prairies, while my people are few, and resemble the scattering trees of a storm-swept plain."[156] Was this happening to Smith's "tribe": "Old Seattle"? Was he indirectly comparing Seathl's experience to the circumstances surrounding the citizens of Seattle? Perhaps, for by the time the speech appeared in the *Seattle Sunday Times* in 1887, the citizens of Seattle had experienced one of the most violent, political unsettling periods of Seattle's history.

Preceding this period, Seattle had grown from a town of 3600 in 1880 to 8000 or more by 1884,[157] but that growth ended in the general business depression of 1884-86. With many businesses going bankrupt, unemployment remained high among white males. They found themselves in competition for jobs with the Chinese. Times were hard, with no end in sight.[158]

---

[155] Arthur A Denny, *Pioneer Days on the Puget Sound*, (Seattle: C.B. Bagley, Printer, 1888), 16. Hereafter cited in the text as Denny, *Pioneer Days*.

[156] Smith, *Seattle Star*, 7.

[157] Nesbit, *Judge Burke*, 55. "The population of Washington and Oregon swelled, increasing faster than the population of the nation as a whole. The few original urban centers grew prodigiously, and new towns sprang up almost overnight. Strangers, whom the old settlers would have never encountered on the Oregon Trail--Scandinavians, Finns, Germans by the thousands--poured into the region." Tyler, *Rebels of the Woods*, 2.

[158] "For months the times have been bad. The peculiar industries of the region are all depressed. . . . The inevitable consequence follows. . . . Our towns are full of idle men. . . . " The *Seattle Call* a newspaper that claimed to represent the laboring man referred to Chinese as "the two-bit conscience of a scurvy opium fiend. . . the treacherous almond-eyed sons of Confucious [sic]. . . clattering round-mouth lepers. . . those yellow rascals who have infested our western country." *Seattle Call*, 17 September 1885, quoted in Daniels, *Anti-Chinese Violence*, 105; Winther, *The Great Northwest*, 423; Nesbit, *Judge Burke*, 172-3; David Suffia, "An early era of ill-feeling," *Seattle Times*, 12 March 1973, 13 (A). Hereafter cited in the text as Suffia, "era of ill-feeling."

On the night of September 5, 1885, tensions between the white laborers and Chinese exploded. A gang of whites and Indians attacked an encampment of Chinese hop-pickers. They killed three Chinese and injured others. Organized agitation began soon after the murders of the hop-pickers. On Sunday, September 20 the Liberal League, an organization of workingmen, called the first mass meeting to rid Seattle of the Chinese. By the time the meeting was over they had formed the Puget Sound anti-Chinese Congress. The vast majority of people who were part of the Puget Sound anti-Chinese Congress were working class. The Seattle businessmen and professionals, who considered themselves as the "better element" or "better class" of citizens, began to voice concern over this growing unrest and anti-capitalist tone of the Puget Sound anti-Chinese Congress. This group held a meeting three days later in the "interests of Law and Order" according to Mayor Henry L. Yesler.[159]

By October, only a month after the gang of whites and Indians had killed the hop-pickers, the situation in Seattle was rapidly deteriorating. The law and order supporters who became known as the Opera House Party began to fear the formation of a conspiracy going far beyond the Chinese question--a conspiracy of capital versus labor. The rhetoric of some of the anti-Chinese leaders only inflamed these fears. One of the local newspapers recorded some the speeches given at the October 3 Puget Sound anti-Chinese Congress meeting:

> The war between capital and labor is coming. Politicians do not like it because it breaks up their slates. . . .

> . . . I don't know how it will be settled. It may be by the destruction of valuable property. I hope not; but it is coming like a war. There is an element of poison in the body politic, which must be removed. . . .

---

[159]The workingmen denounced the meeting of these "prominent" citizens "as the adherents of 'capital and monopoly.'" *Seattle Call*, 5 October 1885, quoted in Daniels, *Anti-Chinese Violence*, 108. Bagley, *History of Seattle*, 458.

. . I understand the parties on the other side [Opera House Party] have elected a vigilance committee to do away with our leaders.[160]

The supporters of law and order based their apprehension on more than just the local politics. The political unrest was not limited to the Pacific Northwest. Their fears were well-founded because of the nationwide populist movement.[161] In a number of areas populists and socialists were gaining power among the working class. There were many strikes in the 1880s, some quite violent.[162] For the 'better element' of Seattle this was significant. They not only saw their own local politics in the throes of anarchy, but they saw their local problems reflected in the growing turmoil throughout the United States.[163] This fueled their trepidation that not only was Seattle in danger, but indeed the entire country was threatened.

By the middle of the 1880s labor's political power was growing.[164] They derisively spoke of the "propertied elite" as the "dog-salmon aristocracy." "Populists who were victorious in the [1886] county elections talked of hanging the 'dog-salmon aristocrats,' and pioneers were roundly criticized as selfish, shortsighted obstacles to progress."[165] The "wagon-train aristocracy":

> clung to its values of hardy enterprise, agrarian simplicity and equality, self-reliance and individualism. . . . . it could not help but grow anxious over the cultural

---

[160] Bagley, *Scrapbook*, No. 5, 128. The newspaper did not identify the speakers.

[161] The local and state populist movement is not to be confused with the national political movement that was represented by the Omaha Convention of 1892.

[162] In the spring of 1886 workers struck nationwide for an eight-hour day and a railroad strike tied up the entire Southwest all the way to St. Louis. "From 1881 to 1885, strikes had averaged about 500 each year, involving 150,000 workers. In 1886 there were over 1,400 strikes, involving 500,000 workers." Howard Zinn, *A People's History of the United States* (New York: Harper & Row, 1980), 267.

[163] An editorial in Seattle's *Post Intelligencer* spoke of the strife in "Chicago, Pittsburgh, the Hocking Valley, and other industrial areas where 'bands of armed men in the avowed socialistic principles' were perfecting themselves in the arts of civil war. . . . *The Post Intelligencer* looked into the future with gloom and foretold that if the year 1885 passed without serious and prolonged labor troubles in the United States 'all ordinary signs shall have failed.'" Wynne, *Reaction to the Chinese*, 213.

[164] Buerge, "Seattle's King Arthur," 28.

[165] Buerge, "Man Who Invented," 23.

changes such progress wrought. The older values . . . of early . . . Washington founders, became, in fact, less and less appropriate to the new urban and industrial society.[166]

A number of disenfranchised working people believed the 'propertied elite' did not represent them. These people and members of the Knights of Labor formed the People's Party. In one of their meetings they "declared that the existing mayor and city council represented a group overly conservative and too much concerned with protecting the interests of the 'old' families--those who had come first to Seattle."[167] Part of their campaign rhetoric painted the original pioneers as "old mossbacks" whose time had long since past. These allegations echo words spoken by the People's Ticket in the election of 1884 when they demanded reform because times had changed and "the older values . . . [were] less and less appropriate to the new urban and industrial society."[168]

As the 1886 election approached even the Seattle leaders of the Knights of Labor feared the situation was getting out of control.[169] The *Post-Intelligencer* published an editorial warning that to vote for the Democrats in the upcoming election amounted to voting for some of the very same men "whose object is the overthrow of our institutions, whose hope is the destruction of our Government, whose triumph would rob you--you, fellow citizens--of home, of country and of religion."[170] It is important not to overlook the fact that this was

---

[166]Tyler, *Rebels of the Woods*, 2.

[167]Avery, *History and Government*, 196.

[168]Tyler, *Rebels of the Woods*, 2.

[169] On April 28, the leaders telegraphed President Cleveland urging him to countermand his order to withdraw troops who had originally been sent to Seattle to quell the anti-Chinese riots. An "armed party drilling daily and declaring loudly to carry coming elections by force if necessary. Threatens lives and property of defenseless citizens." Judge Roger S. Greene of Seattle believed the Chinese issue was only a side issue and was being "used as a pretext for socialistic outbreaks." George Kinnear wrote that as soon as the troops were withdrawn the anti-Chinese sympathizers, "began to organize an armed force to take possession of the City and shoot down any armed opposition. . . . our men [city leaders] declared that if they had to meet an armed mob they would shoot down every one they could find. . . . If their [anti-Chinese sympathizers] plan succeeded, they were to arrest a number of our leading men, convict and hang them." Kinnear, *Anti-Chinese Riots*, 11.

[170]*Post-Intelligencer*, 12 July 1886, 1.

election year rhetoric and that this newspaper "was normally orthodox in its Republicanism. . . ."[171] But the warning only underscores the pervasive fear felt by the conservative populace.

In the Seattle municipal elections in July of 1886 the People's Party prevailed.[172] The very same group that earlier The *Post-Intelligencer* had warned want "the overthrow of our institutions, . . . rob you . . . of home, of country and of religion."[173] The party opposing the People's Party, the Loyal League, "lost every race except the Council elections in the second and third districts."[174] This highlights again that facts, not just rumors and exaggerations, created this apprehension among the original pioneers.

This climate of social unrest throughout the country, the revolution in Seattle's city politics and the disparagement of the original pioneers seems to have prompted Dr. Smith to begin writing a series of reminiscences of the "old days," the days of the original pioneers. Only three of these have been found in their entirety: Number Nine on Governor Stevens, Number Ten on Chief Seathl and Number Eleven subtitled "The Roll of Honor." "The Roll of Honor" was a series of short paragraphs on Seattle's pioneers not mentioned in the other ten reminiscences. Smith's writings may have been an attempt to remind these newly arrived emigrants—"New Seattle"--of the hardships and the sacrifices endured by the pioneers. David Buerge believes that:

> Chief Seattle's speech . . . was a peroration on the experience of change as endured by the Indians and as pioneers themselves now faced. The speech described a profoundly different experience than what Americans liked to imagine was their destiny. . . It was a prophecy, the publication suggested, that could apply as well to those who threatened the dog-salmon aristocrats.[175]

---

[171]Nesbit, *Judge Burke*, 85.

[172]The People's Party slate won by forty-one votes. Avery, *History and Government*, 196. The Party was not successful in the territorial elections. A group of like-minded Democrats were able to take control of the Democratic Convention and have it adopt an anti-Chinese resolution--the defining issue for the People's Party.

[173]*Post-Intelligencer*, 12 July 1886, 1.

[174]Daniels, *Anti-Chinese Violence*, 128.

[175]Buerge, "Seattle's King Arthur," 29.

When Smith quotes Seathl lamenting his peoples' loss, Smith appears to be speaking of the fate befallen the "dog-salmon aristocracy" that controlled the politics of Seattle for over thirty years:[176]

> I will not mourn over our untimely decay, nor reproach my pale-face brothers for hastening it, for we, too, may have been somewhat to blame. . . .
>
> . . . No, we are two distinct races and must ever remain so. There is little in common between us. The ashes of our ancestors are sacred and their final resting place is hallowed ground, while you wander away from the tombs of your fathers seemingly without regret. . . .
>
> . . . But why should we repine? Why should I murmur at the fate of my people? Tribes are made up of individuals and are no better than they. Men come and go like the waves of the sea. A tear, a tamanawus, a dirge, and they are gone from our longing eyes forever. Even the white man, whose God walked and talked with him, as friend to friend is not exempt from the common destiny. We may be brothers after all. We shall see.[177]

The Seattle election of 1886 was a victory for the Populist ticket. They successfully defeated those who protected "the interests of the 'old' families." [178] The day after the election one newspaper published an editorial saying, "It believes, as it has repeatedly said, that this was no ordinary election, and it believes now that the revolt in its [the word was illegible] effects will be no ordinary result."[179]

The defeated mayoral candidate, Arthur A. Denny, an original pioneer, wrote his memoirs saying that ". . . I think it by no means improper for any of the few settlers now left, who maybe so disposed,

---

[176]Not only was Smith an original pioneer, but he was an active conservative politician being a member of the Republican party since it was originally organized. He was elected four times to the lower house of the legislature. Bagley, *History of Seattle*, 267.

[177]Smith, *Seattle Star*, 7.

[178]Avery, *History and Government*, 196.

[179]*Post-Intelligencer*, 13 July 1886, p. 1.

to contribute what they can to make a record, which must now be very quickly done if done at all."[180] Denny went on to make caustic remarks about these "degenerate scrubs":

> all who came to Oregon in the early times . . . fully earned all they got, but we have a small class of (*very small*) people here now who have no good word for the old settler that so bravely met every danger. . . These, however are degenerate scrubs, too cowardly to face the same dangers that our pioneer men and women did, and too lazy to perform an honest day's work. . . .[181]
> and I will presume to say that if the people now possessed more of the spirit that then actuated the "old mossbacks," as some reproachedly style the old settlers, we would hear less about conflict between labor and capital, which in truth is largely a conflict between labor and laziness. We had no eight hour, nor ten hour days then, and I never heard of any one striking, not even an Indian. . . [182]

Henry Yesler, who had been the mayor for two terms and one of the original venture capitalists in Seattle, also "scratched out a few pages of memories."[183] It was in this political and literary climate that Smith wrote his series of eleven reminiscences of the pioneer days: "Among his pioneer contemporaries who nurtured literary pretensions, Henry Smith was the most attuned to the transient nature of their accomplishments."[184]

Smith published the speech at end of Seattle's tumultuous times. The 'better elements,' who had been in power since the founding of Seattle, were soundly defeated in the election of 1886. Seattle was in the midst of what one newspaper considered a revolution. They wrote that the People's Party's "object is the overthrow of our institutions. . . [their] hope is the destruction of our Government."[185] The original

---

[180]Denny, *Pioneer Days,* 4.

[181]Ibid., 16.

[182]Ibid., 27.

[183]Buerge, "Man Who Invented," 23.

[184]Ibid., 19.

[185]*Post-Intelligencer,* 12 July 1886, 1.

pioneers found themselves denounced as "obstacles in the way of progress," as "old mossbacks" and the rhetoric became so hot that some sinophobes spoke of hanging them.

Seathl's speech anticipates the feelings of the "old mossbacks" considered "obstacles to progress" and whose time had long passed when he said:

> There was a time when our people covered the whole land, as the waves of a wind-ruffled sea cover its shell-paved floor. But that time has long since passed away with the greatness of tribes now almost forgotten.[186]

But even though that greatness was "almost forgotten" in the closing lines of his speech, Seathl said his people would never leave this land even when dead:

> And when the last red man shall have perished from the earth and his memory among white man shall have become a myth, these shores shall swarm with the invisible dead of my tribe, and when your children's children shall think themselves alone in the field, the store, the shop, upon the highway or in the silence of the woods they will not be alone. In all the earth there is no place dedicated to solitude. At night, when the streets of your cities and villages shall be silent, and you think them deserted, they will throng with the returning hosts that once filled and still love this beautiful land. The white man will never be alone. Let him be just and deal kindly with my people, for the dead are not altogether powerless.[187]

Are these the words of Smith or Seathl? Is Smith speaking of "Old Seattle's" demise? Are these Seathl's words that simply reflect the feelings of Smith and his fellow pioneers? Are the sentiments of Seathl appropriate for the trials Smith and his friends had been through and were still experiencing? One can only speculate.

---

[186]Smith, *Seattle Star*, 7.
[187]Ibid.

Seathl's speech did lament the passing of the Indians. It spoke of the white man's future realization of his error. It did not speak of the wonders of progress, but spoke of the cyclical rise and fall of men: "Men come and go like the waves of the sea." It spoke of the sacredness of the natural world and the importance of their ancestors that had lived here from the beginning of time: "Every hill-side, every valley, every plain and grove has been hallowed by some fond memory or sad experience of my tribe." Although the "hallowness" of nature was more Smith's perspective than that of the local capitalists, was he pointing out the difference in how the early settlers and the new emigrants related to the land? Was Smith hoping to use Seathl as an example to prove that the People's Party and their ilk would soon pass as Seathl's people had? The newly elected now thought of themselves as powerful, but would their time soon come to an end and their greatness be "forgotten?" Seathl's people had once thought themselves powerful and had "covered the whole land, as the waves of a wind-ruffled sea cover its shell-paved floor. . . .," but those times came to an end; "time has long since passed away with the greatness of tribes now almost forgotten." Certainly, Seathl's words parallel Smith's sentiments. Is it a coincidence that Smith wrote these eleven reminiscences after the election of 1886 joining two of his fellow "mossbacks" who also wrote their pioneer memoirs and took potshots at the newly elected? There is a strong inferential case that these factors--the depression of 1884, the anti-Chinese riots, the socialistic/anarchistic rhetoric, the election of 1886 and the disparagement of the original pioneers--influenced the writing and publication of the speech.

The answer to the question as to why Smith delayed publishing the speech will remain unclear. The political and economic events appear to have played a significant role in prompting Smith to publish it. However, there is another very important question: the accuracy of Smith's version. No one has uncovered any other writings that document Seathl's words that day. There are three other speeches by Seathl that were recorded: two by government officials and one by an early pioneer B. F. Shaw.

Chapter IV

Chief Seathl's Recorded Speeches

There is no question that Smith's version was not a word-for-word translation of Seathl's speech. There are three different speeches given by Seathl that are documented. Government officials recorded two of these. The third was a speech given to a group of American explorers who visited Seathl's village. The speeches bear no resemblance to the Victorian prose of Smith's version.

Government officials recorded Seathl's speech at the Point Elliott Treaty and the lament spoken to the Indian Agent for the Puget Sound District, Colonel Michael T. Simmons. B. F. Shaw also recorded a speech Seathl delivered to him and a party of fellow explorers when they first arrived on the shores of Seathl's village in 1850. In comparison to Smith's version, these three recorded speeches are quite different in diction and syntax.

The National Archives has the notes of the treaty proceedings at Point Elliott. Seathl spoke little. There are only a few paragraphs in the notes of the proceedings, but these few paragraphs give insight into *how he spoke*. On January 22, 1855, during the treaty signing Stevens asked: "Does anyone object to what I have said? Does my venerable friend Seathl object? I want Seathl to give his will to me and speak to his people." Seathl answered:

> I look upon you as my father. I and the rest regard you as such. All of the Indians have the same good feeling towards you and will send it on paper to the Great Father. All of them, men, women and children rejoice that he has sent you to take care of them. My mind is like yours. I don't want to say more. My heart is very

good towards Dr. Maynard [a physician who was present]. I want always to get medicine from him.[188]

The next day during the treaty Seathl spoke again:

> Seattle then on behalf of himself and the other Chiefs brought a white flag and presented it saying: "Now by this we make friends and put away all bad feelings if we ever had any. We look upon you as our father. We will never change our minds, but since you have been to see us we will be always the same. Now, do you send this paper of our hearts to the Great Chief. That is all I have to say."[189]

The speech Seathl gave to Colonel Simmons, the Indian Agent, in May 15, 1858, also was recorded. Colonel Simmons was visiting the various tribes to listen to their grievances. By this time the people in Puget Sound considered Simmons the "Daniel Boone of the territory" having brought the first settlers to the Sound in 1844.[190] In 1858 the U.S. Senate still had not ratified the Treaty of Point Elliott and the failure of ratification had left the Indian tribes impoverished and hostile. Simmons spoke Chinook jargon and had a "mastery of Indian languages and . . . knowledge of Indian psychology,"[191] so he was able to converse without an interpreter. With Simmons came the editor of the *Pioneer and Democrat* newspaper who took notes of the journey and later published his account of the expedition. The editor wrote that during the meeting with Seathl, Simmons gave a "short but very

---

[188][Notes of the treaty proceedings of the Treaty of Mukilteo or Point Elliott], Treaty of Mukilteo or Point Elliott, Treaty Papers 1854 & 1855, 9, Microfilm Frame No. 285, (Documents Relating to the Negotiations of Ratified and Unratified Treaties with Various Indian Tribes, 1801-69. T-494. 10 rolls), (National Archives Microfilm Publications T494, roll 5), Records of the Bureau of Indian affairs Record Group; 75, National Archives, Washington, D.C. Hereafter cited in the text as "Treaty proceedings of the Treaty of Mukilteo or Point Elliott."

[189]"Treaty proceedings of the Treaty of Mukilteo or Point Elliott," 11, Microfilm Frame 287; Stevens, *Life of Stevens*, 463-466.

[190]Cantwell, *Hidden Northwest*, 97. Stevens spoke of him as "one of the oldest settlers, if not the American pioneer . . . a kind, frank, confiding man, of excellent judgment, and strong sense." Ibid., 98.

[191]Cantwell, *Hidden Northwest*, 98.

appreciative speech telling them that he had not forgotten them; that they must not be discouraged or become melancholy because their treaties had not been concluded . . . [he also] admonished them about drinking liquor."[192] The following is Seathl's lament that in part may have been sparked by Simmon's comment concerning the tribe's liquor consumption.

I am not a bad man; I want you to understand what I say; I do not drink rum; neither does New-E-Chis, [another chief present] and we continually advise our people not to do so.

I am and always have been a friend to the whites. I listen to what Mr. Page (the resident agent) says to me, and I do not steal nor do any of my people steal from the whites.

Oh, Mr. Simmons, why do not our papers come back to us? You always say they will come back, but they do not come. I fear that we are forgotten or that we are to be cheated out of our land.

I have been very poor and hungry all winter and am very sick now. In a little while I will die. I should like to be paid for my lands before I die. Many of my people died during the cold winter without getting their pay. When I die my people will be very poor - they will have no property, no chief and no one to talk for them. You must not forget them, Mr. Simmons, when I am gone.

We are ashamed when we think of the Puyallups, as they have now got their papers. They fought against the whites whilst we, who have never been angry with them, get nothing. When we get our pay we want it in money. The Indians are not bad. It is the mean white men that are bad to them. If any person writes that we do not want our papers they tell lies.

Oh, Mr. Simmons; you see I am sick, I want you to write quickly to the great chief what I say. I am done. [193]

[192] Bagley, *History of Seattle*, 93.

[193] Costello, *Legends and Tales*, 111-2; Bagley, *History of Seattle*, 93-4.

Comparing Seathl's diction and syntax in the notes of the Treaty of Point Elliott and the lament to Smith's version, a first reading evokes questions as to the authenticity of Smith's version. These are a few sentences from Smith's transcripts:

> Yonder sky that has wept tears of compassion on our fathers for centuries untold, and which, to us, looks eternal, may change.

> They still love its winding rivers, its great mountains and its sequestered vales, and they ever yearn in tenderest affection over the lonely hearted living and often return to visit and comfort them.

> Sad-voiced winds moan in the distance. Some grim Nemesis of our race is on the red man's trail, and wherever he goes he will still hear the sure approaching footsteps of the fell destroyer and prepare to meet his doom, as the wounded doe that hears the approaching footsteps of the hunter.

> The sable braves, and fond mothers, and glad-hearted maidens, and the little children who lived and rejoiced here, and whose very names are now forgotten, still love these solitudes, and their deep fastnesses at eventide grow shadowy with the presence of dusky spirits.[194]

The flowery prose is closer to Victorian oratory than to Lushosteed, the language of Seathl's people and a dialect of Salish. It is hard to believe the Chief of the Duwamish and Suquamish with no Western education would speak in such a style.[195] The speech reflects the

---

[194]Smith, *Seattle Star*, 7.

[195]William Arrowsmith, Baltimore, to Mary-Thadia D'Hondt, Seattle, 17 July 1980, Museum of History and Industry, Seattle, Washington. Hereafter cited in the text as Arrowsmith to D'Hondt. Dr. Arrowsmith was a professor in Classical Studies and translated Smith's version from Victorian prose to a style of speaking that was a closer rendition of how Seathl may have spoken.

"Victorian age of florid literature and customs."[196] The speech given at the treaty proceedings and the lament are more indicative of speeches filtered through a trade patois of five hundred words than Smith's version.

Most authors who have written about Seathl agree that he did not speak English and he definitely could not write in English. Some have said that he most likely knew Chinook jargon, but disliked it and refused to use it.[197] Sam Coombs said, "Though a man of great natural abilities, Chief Sealth never learned either Chinook or the English languages; nor did the older Indians whom I knew."[198] William Arrowsmith was a prominent and highly respected Classical Studies professor at Boston University and the first person to translate the speech from the Victorian prose of Smith to a closer rendition of how Seathl may have spoken.[199] Arrowsmith said in a letter to Carl Ross, one of the first Europeans to trace the authenticity of the environmental speech, "Seattle's English was minimal" and that he probably delivered it "in his native Duwamish."[200] Vanderwerth, who compiled a book on Native American speeches that included historian Clarence Bagley's reworking of Smith's version, wrote that "the speech was delivered through an interpreter"[201] If this was the case, it was first translated into Chinnock Jargon and then English. John M. Rich introduced the speech to Bagley, rewrote his own version of the speech and published it in 1931. He edited Smith's version by omitting some of Smith's words and phrases and adding his own. Rich wrote that Seathl "conveyed his thoughts in the dignified, picturesque, Indian language."[202] Arrowsmith wrote to Janice Krenmayr, the first journalist to expose the fraudulent environmental speech attributed to Seathl,

---

[196] Krenmayr, "The earth." 6.

[197] Ibid. 4.

[198] Sam Coombs quoted in Costello, *Life Legends and Tales*, 105.

[199] Before he died in 1992 Arrowsmith was a "professor at Boston University in Classical Studies, a scholar of the classics, translator of languages and author of many books with many awards and fellowships to his credit." Krenmayr, "The earth," 6.

[200] William Arrowsmith, [no city or state given], to Carl Ross, [no city, state or country given], 20 January 1978, quoted in Kaiser, "Seattle Speech(es)," 505. Hereafter cited in the text as Arrowsmith to Ross, 1978.

[201] Vanderwerth, *Oratory*, 119.

[202] Rich, *Challenge*, 18. He never explained why he took such poetic license with Smith's original version. For a more detailed discussion of this matter see Chapter V. "Clarence B. Bagley's and John M. Rich's Versions of the Speech" 46.

saying "Rich had merely tacked more nonsense onto Smith's version . . . . . What Rich added was indeed worthless . . ."[203] Replying to an inquiry by Carl Ross, Arrowsmith wrote in 1978, "I incline to think that much of Smith's version was authentic." This confirmed his assertion in the *American Poetry Review* (1975) that "the speech in Smith's version evidently followed the original closely."[204] Two years later in a letter to Ms. Mary-Thadia D'Hondt, archivist librarian for the Seattle Historical Society, Arrowsmith said, "In my opinion, there's a possibility that part of the speech, a nucleus, may actually have been spoken by Seattle and transcribed by Smith."[205] He later changed his mind. By 1989 he was seriously questioning the authenticity of the entire speech. In a letter to Dan and Pat Miller, who were researching the origins of the various speeches, he wrote:

> we have a real problem of authenticity . . . . It's my view that Smith made a few handwritten notes at the time of the speech and than put them aside. . . . embellishing it thickly with texts that inhabited the white man's cultural memory.[206]

Arrowsmith had found references in Smith's version from the Bible, Milton, Emerson, Bryon, Jonathan Edwards, Cotton Mather, and several others.[207] He was planning on publishing an article that outlined a number of other references from classical writers that Smith used in his transcribing of Seathl's speech.[208] Arrowsmith died before he had a

---

[203] Arrowsmith, Boston, to Janice Krenmayr, Seattle, 6 January 1975, Museum of History and Industry, Seattle, Washington. Hereafter cited in the text as Arrowsmith to Krenmayr, 1975.

[204] Arrowsmith to Ross, 1978.

[205] Arrowsmith to D'Hondt, 1980.

[206] Arrowsmith, to Miller, 26 November 1989, 2.

[207] Professor William Arrowsmith, interview by the author, 1 December 1992, Sebastopol Ca., telephone. Hereinafter cited as Arrowsmith, 1 December 1992; "a textual analysis done by Wm. Arrowsmith and others suggest that it was probably written by a white man who knew Milton, the Bible, etc." Ted Perry, Middlebury Vermont, to the author, Sebastopol, California, 25 October 1991, Museum of History and Industry, Seattle, Washington; Arrowsmith, to Miller, 26 November 1989, 2.

[208] Arrowsmith, 1 December 1992.

chance to write the article. All his work is being held by the Special Collections at the Boston University Library.[209]

The language of Seathl's people had its own beauty, but they did not use the metaphors and similes of Victorian prose. Krenmayr wrote

> those who live here [Seattle] and grew up, as it were, steeping themselves in the beauty of the good Dr. Smith's phrases, will counter: Who is to know, without being fluent in Seattle's native tongue that it too, was not more like a native 'Victorian' style? And Smith tried to do justice as nearly as possible?[210]

There are early Salishian "dictionaries" that include Seathl's language and they clearly show:

> Smith's whole speech is, in fact, jampacked with Victorian fustian of the same sort---words for which no equivalents exist in any Indian language I know of. This is of course emphatically <u>not</u> to say that Indian languages aren't capable of great an eloquent language---true poetry---simply that the eloquence is not that of Senator Claghorn or his Victorian predecessor. <u>Fustian</u> simply no part of Indian eloquence. Indian eloquence is indeed quite complex (as almost all poetry of primitives is, though to us it looks deceptively simple) but its complexity is a matter of richly inflected thought; evocative and patterned repetition; the formal structure of poetry (even where the speaker is speaking what we would call 'prose').[211]

---

[209] All of Arrowsmith's work is at the Special Collections at Boston University Library and as of December 1996 they were unable to locate the specific unpublished article or notes for an article on Smith's references to classical writers. But Arrowsmith did ask this author to not "jump the gun" and publish Arrowsmith's findings until Arrowsmith could publish his article. Arrowsmith, 1 December 1992. He also asked Daniel Miller to not "jump the gun" back in 1989. Daniel Miller, interview by the author, 19 November 1996, Sebastopol, California, telephone.

[210] Krenmayr, "The earth," 6.

[211] Arrowsmith to Krenmayr, 1975.

67

Clarence Bagley, a well-respected Pacific Northwest historian at the turn of the century, concluded his reworking of Smith's version with, "Doubtless Chief Seattle . . . expressed its thought and sentiments in their own language forming the thread of speech, but to Doctor Smith belongs the credit for its beautiful wording and delightful imagery."[212]

Before Arrowsmith translated Seathl's speech, he spent time in the Seattle area among the Native Americans who follow the more traditional ways of their culture. He was trying to get a sense of how they may have phrased their words and thoughts in 1854.[213]

He translated Smith's version only after years of "reading Indian treaty negotiations, Indian speeches, etc. for my book, of what---if Smith's version is accurate---Seattle presumably said."[214] He tried to "think 'under'"[215] the Victorian verbosity of the speech and glean the nucleus of what Seathl may have been saying.

Without the notes Smith claimed to have taken, it is impossible to know whether his version accurately restates Seathl's words or even if there are fragments of Seathl's thoughts reflected in Smith's version. Buerge believes that although the Victorian oratory found in the speech is the writing of Smith, "the notes Smith claimed he took during the speech are an authentic transmission of beliefs about the time of year in which it was given and about the larger crisis confronting the Indian people, whose world was threatened with profound change."[216] There are a number of references in Smith's version that parallel the beliefs of the Native Americans of the Puget Sound about the dead and the season.

Most Northwest Coast Indians divided the year between two seasons: the summer and winter. They devoted summer to secular

---

[212]Bagley, "Angeline," 255.

[213]One of the traditional people he spoke with was Dorothy Newton, the great granddaughter of Chief Seathl. She said her father, the grandson of Chief Seathl, refused to use the white man's terminology. For example, when his car had a flat tire he would say, "My canoe has a broken leg." This gives a sense of how one of the descendants of Seathl, a grandson, who had little use for American English terminology, used English. Arrowsmith, 1 December.

[214]Arrowsmith to D'Hondt, 1980.

[215]Arrowsmith to D'Hondt, 1980.

[216]Buerge, "Seattle's King Arthur," 28.

activities and winter to the sacred.[217] They believed that in the winter there was an open door between the land of the dead and the living: "this spirit came close to its human partner every winter. . ."[218] "And your power calls by and sees you every winter. I don't know why, but tama`namis comes strong in the winter. Every winter your power will come to you and make you sick and you have to sing and feed it and dance with it . . ."[219] The dead would walk among them, some visiting and some stealing the souls of the living. During the winter shamans would hold elaborate Soul Recovery ceremonies to return the kidnapped souls of the living.

> The ceremony was always held at night during the midwinter, our months of December or January. Because many, if not all, of the features of the land of the dead were the reverse of those in this world, the journey was easy, and safe, and enjoyable. A winter night in this world was a bright, pretty, summer day in the afterworld. The path was unobstructed passing through many colorful flowers.[220]

Throughout Smith's version Seathl makes references to the dead and their love of their homeland.

---

[217]"The patterns of group membership, of the individual's identification with a larger social whole, the bonds of kinship and friendship that operate in the summer are in effect only then; at the start of the [winter] ceremonies that mark the oneset of the sacred season, they become secondary to those between the individual humans and individual spirits." Stanley Walens, *Feasting with Cannibals: An Essay on Kwakiutl Cosmology* (Princeton, New Jersey: Princeton University Press, 1981), 44. Among the Kwakiutl, their winter ceremonies were so serious that "even simple mistakes made during ritual performances at the winter ceremonials may be punished by death; at the very least the giving of a potlatch . . ." Ibid., 41.

[218]Jay Miller, ed., *Mourning Dove: A Salishan Autobiography,* (Lincoln, Nebraska: University of Nebraska Press, 1990), 123; Wayne Suttles, *Coast Salish Essays,* (Seattle: University of Washington Press, 1987), 200-4.

[219]From an interview in 1940 with Frank Allen, a Skokomish Indian by William W. Elmendorf. Elmendorf, *Twana Narratives* (41.3), 165.

[220]Jay Miller, *Shamanic Odyssey: The Lushootseed Salish Journey to the Land of the Dead* (Menlo Park, California: Ballena Press), 1988, 9. For a eyewitness account of a Suquamish Soul Recovery ceremony see Ibid., 33-7.

[Ancestors] who lived and rejoiced here, and whose very names are now forgotten, still love these solitudes, and their deep fastnesses at eventide grow shadowy with the presence of dusky spirits. And when the last red man shall have perished from the earth and his memory among white man shall have become a myth, these shores shall swarm with the invisible dead of my tribe, and when your children's children shall think themselves alone in the field, the store, the shop, upon the highway or in the silence of the woods they will not be alone.[221]

"The chaos resulting from depopulation produced religious leaders who prophesied the imminent return of the dead."[222] Smith's version reflects these beliefs.

There is an oral tradition among the elders of the Squamish tribe that Smith began working on the speech eight months after Seathl spoke and "worked really hard on it to get it as accurate as he could."[223] According to that tradition, he collaborated with Seathl over a five-year period to assure its accuracy. There is no other documentation to verify their collaboration either by acquaintances or in the reminiscences of Smith's daughter.[224]

In the 1980s, the Suquamish began recording oral histories from their grandparents and great grandparents. Oral histories are "representations of the past in the present. One cannot deny either the past or the present in them . . . Traditions must always be understood

---

[221]Smith, *Seattle Star*, 7.

[222]Buerge, "Seattle's King Arthur," 28.

[223]Marilyn Jones, curator for the Suquamish Museum in Suquamish, Washington, interview by author, 12 November 1992, Sebastopol, California, telephone.

[224]For a detailed discussion of this matter see Ione Smith Graff, "Memoirs of Dr. Henry A. Smith," 1957, Seattle Museum of History and Industry, Seattle, Washington. For a more detailed discussion on the role oral traditions play in historical research see Appendix 14, Jan Vansina, *Oral Tradition As History* (Madison, Wisconsin: University of Wisconsin Press, 1985). Hereinafter cited in the text as Vansina, *Oral Tradition*, and *A Study in Historical Methodology*, trans. H. M. Wright (Chicago: Aldine Publishing Co., 1961).

as reflecting both the past and the present in a single breath."[225] The elders were familiar only with Smith's transcription. The Suquamish had passed Smith's version down through the generations as the speech given by Seathl. The recorders had a "minimum of five elders" read Smith's speech and "the elders verified" it as the speech that was passed down orally. The elders were unaware of any other versions of the speech. They understood that Smith's notes and original speech were lost when a barn burned down on Smith's property.[226] The elders verification of the speech places Smith's version as the "authentic traditional speech" or, at the least, it is the message caged in Victorian terminology. His notes may have been lost in the Great Seattle Fire when Smith's office, not his barn, burned down.[227]

There is little doubt as to whether Smith's version is a word for word rendition of Seathl's speech. It is not. Seathl's rhetoric was not the Victorian locution and eloquence found in Smith's writing. The florid Victorian terminology found in Smith's version is Smith's alone. The enigma is whether Smith's version reflects any of the thoughts, emotions, beliefs, fears and hopes that Seathl tried to convey to Governor Stevens. At the time of Professor Arrowsmith's death he concluded that the entire speech was a concoction of Smith's imagination and knowledge of classical literature. He died before he was able to publish his reasons for this conclusion.[228] In a letter to Daniel Miller, Arrowsmith wrote a summation of why he thought the speech was the words of Smith and not Seathl.

---

[225] Jan Vansina, *Oral Tradition As History* (Madison, Wisconsin: University of Wisconsin Press, 1985), xii. See also: *A Study in Historical Methodology,* trans. H. M. Wright (Chicago: Aldine Publishing Co., 1961).

[226] All of the information in this paragraph is based on notes from a telephone conversation between the author and Marilyn Jones, the curator for the Suquamish Museum in Suquamish, Washington. Marilyn Jones, interview by author, 12 November 1992, Sebastopol, California, telephone. The interviews of elders can be found at the Suquamish Museum in Suquamish, Washington.

[227] Buerge, 9 February. The six ledgers full of his poetry and writing, may have been lost in this fire too. Ione Smith Graff, "Memoirs of Dr. Henry A. Smith," 1957, 7, Seattle Museum of History and Industry, Seattle, Washington.

[228] He also told Daniel Miller in a conversation back in 1989 that he was planning to publish this article noting all the references used by Smith. Daniel Miller, interview by author, 17 November 1996, Sebastopol, California, telephone.

If you believe that the speech as reported by Smith is substantially what Seattle actually said, then how do you explain the allusions, the echoes and quotations from the classics . . . echoes in it from, among others: Byron, Emerson, Milton, Jonathan Edwards, etc.? . . . phrases which tally exactly with the words of Byron et al. Take, for instance, that vivid phrase in the Smith speech: "the iron finger of an angry God," What I hear in both the substance of the paragraph and the actual words of is the echo of Jonathan Edwards' notorious sermon, "Sinners in the Hands of an Angry God," . . . there are so many embellishments, and their purpose (if indeed they are, as I suspect, quite conscious allusions---a tip to the educated among readers) . . . What better way to arouse a sense of conscience in the white man than to have an Indian speak to him in his own classic texts and the values implicit in those texts, all the great texts of human transience: Lo, how the mighty are fallen; pull down thy pride; Vanity, vanity, saith the preacher; For the days of man are like the leaves (or the grass or flowers); Be gentle, for your time may come (and we may be brothers after all). . . ?[229]

David Buerge, on the other hand, has come to believe that

> the notes Smith claimed he took during the speech are an authentic transmission of beliefs about that time of year in which it was given and about the larger crisis confronting the Indian people, whose world was threatened with profound change. . . . [But he qualifies this saying] we cannot be sure about the speech's authenticity.[230]

Whether Smith transmitted the beliefs accurately does not answer the question of whether Seathl spoke of these beliefs. The Bible was the only piece of the classical literature with which Seathl had come into contact. Catholic laymen and priests used Biblical stories to teach Christianity. So there is no doubt that the references to Euro-American

---

[229]Arrowsmith to Miller, 26 November 1989, 1-2.
[230]Buerge, "Seattle's King Arthur," 28.

writers are Smith's additions. What is impossible to know is whether Seathl's voice is underneath the Victorian fustian.

The story of Seathl's speech would have stayed buried in the October 29, 1887, edition of the *Seattle Sunday Star,* an obscure local Seattle newspaper, except for four people: two historians, Frederic James Grant and Clarence B. Bagley; a dentist from the Puget Sound area, John M. Rich and a woman who complied stories from old pioneers into a book, Roberta Frye Watt. Frederic Grant was the first to reprint Smith's version and thirty-eight years later Clarence Bagley published his own personal version of the speech. There is even controversy surrounding Bagley's version because Rich claims Bagley did not know the speech existed until he showed it to Bagley. Watt used Bagley's version of the speech and added a few of her own flourishes.

Chapter V

Clarence B. Bagley and John M. Rich's Versions
of the Speech

Four people were instrumental in keeping Seathl's speech in the public eye after Smith published it in 1887. The first was Frederic Grant who wrote *The History of Seattle*[231] in 1891 and included Smith's version. Three decades later, two men and a woman published the speech, thereby ensuring its place in Puget Sound lore.

Except for a few minor changes in punctuation and the combination of two paragraphs, Frederic Grant's version was the only one to faithfully follow the original version. Twelve years after Grant had published his history, Frank Carlson wrote a thesis for his Master of Arts at the University of Washington titled "Chief Sealth." Although Carlson wrote in the preface: "the aim and object of this thesis is to present a complete and accurate report of the life and achievement of Sealth . . .," there is not a single mention of the speech or of Dr. Smith. [232] Carlson did, however, include Seathl's speech at the treaty proceedings and his speech in 1858 to Michael T. Simmons, an Indian Agent. Carlson even has a chapter titled "Reminiscences of the Whites." As part of his research he interviewed several pioneers and Indians of the Port Madison Reservation. One of the people he interviewed was Clarence B. Bagley, a local historian. But there are no references to the speech Smith published and in Carlson's bibliography

---

[231]Frederic James Grant, *History of Seattle* (New York: American Publishing Co., 1891). For a more detailed discussion of this matter see Appendix 2.

[232]Frank Carlson, *Chief Sealth*. (Seattle: University of Washington Bulletin Series III No. 2, December 1903) 1.

no mention of Frederic Grant's *The History of Seattle*. The speech remained unnoticed for another twenty-six years.

In 1929, Clarence B. Bagley reproduced the speech in his book, *History of King County, Washington* and two years later published it again in an article entitled "Chief Seattle and Angeline" in *Washington Historical Quarterly*. There is no way to know how much Smith adulterated Seathl's words. But we do know that Bagley was the first to adulterate Smith's version and publish his own.

In 1931 Roberta Frye Watt wrote *The Story of Seattle*[233] based on reminiscences from her family and the pioneers of Puget Sound. She included Chief Seathl's speech, but used Bagley's version and making a few changes in his version. There are three letters in the Clarence Bagley Collection from her. In her letter on September 3, 1931, she wrote, "I am writing to ask your permission to quote from your *History of Seattle* in my story of pioneer Seattle. Altho' you have been most generous in your help and have given me permission to use any material in your books. . ."[234] A few weeks later, on the September 21st, she thanked him for his permission. The third letter is undated and she thanked him for sending her the article on Seathl in the *Washington Historical Quarterly*. None of these letters directly refer to Seathl's speech, but it is obvious that Watt edited Bagley's version.[235]

In 1932, the year after Bagley published "Chief Seattle and Angeline," John M. Rich, a local dentist with an interest in Indian lore, wrote a booklet entitled *Chief Seattle's Unanswered Challenge*. He claims to have known of the speech before Bagley. There are three letters from Rich in the papers of Clarence B. Bagley. All three concern Seathl's speech and the fact that Rich was "the first to get it properly to the attention of those in Seattle & elsewhere who appreciate such things."[236] He did not date the first letter, but "[1930?]" appears in the

---

[233]Roberta Frye Watt, *The Story of Seattle* (Portland: Binford & Mort, 1932) 180-82.

[234] Roberta Frye Watt, Seattle Washington, to Clarence B. Bagley, Seattle, Washington, Transcript in the hand of Roberta Frye Watt, 3 September 1931 and 21 September 1931, Clarence Bagley Collection, Manuscripts & University Archives Division, University of Washington, Seattle, Washington.

[235]For a more detailed discussion of this matter see Appendix 5.

[236]John M. Rich, Seattle, Washington, to Clarence B. Bagley, Seattle, Washington, 1930?, Transcript in the hand of John M. Rich, Clarence Bagley Collection, Manuscripts & University Archives Division, University of Washington, Seattle, Washington, 1. Hereafter cited in the text as Rich, Letter "1930?," 255.

upper right-hand corner.[237] This would be one year before Bagley wrote the article, "Chief Seattle and Angeline," for the *Washington Historical Quarterly* and a year after he published his book *History of King County, Washington*. In Rich's letter he states that neither Bagley nor Professor Edmond S. Meany, an eminent Pacific Northwest History professor at Washington State, knew of Smith's version.

> "My dear Mr. Bagley -
> Inside of my feelings about the great speech of Chief Seattle preserved for us by Dr. Smith, is a certain satisfaction of being the first to get it properly to the attention of those in Seattle & elsewhere who appreciate such things.
> I think it true that very few have any idea of the literary and historical value of this address or even know of its existence.
> As I told you *when I discovered it I went to you among the first and found that you and Prof. Meany did not know of its existence - and gave you a copy of it* [emphasis added].
> I have put much study and effort to so present this that it will find a permanent place in Seattle historical collection and *it would please me very much if you would delay your publication of it until after mine comes out* [emphasis added] - for I have been in hopes to be the one calling special attention to it. . . .
> When your history is published I hope this writing of mine will make it even more sought after - If you feel you must allow your copy to appear in the "Quarterly" *I wonder if you would not say before it or somewhere that I called your attention to the speech and I gave you the first copy you had seen?* [emphasis added]. "[238]

Rich's letter raises a number of questions. In 1929, Bagley published Seathl's speech in *The History of King County, Washington*. This is a year before Rich's letter if in fact 1930 is the correct year. Rich did write that when "I discovered it I went to you among the first"[239] so it

---

[237] Ibid., 1.

[238] Ibid., 1-3.

[239] Ibid., 1.

is possible years could have passed between Rich's discovery, his meeting with Bagley and this [1930] letter. It still does not explain Rich's pleading with Bagley not to publish the speech before him or at least to give him credit for the uncovering of the speech. Why bother pleading if he wrote the letter in 1930? If Bagley had already published the speech in 1929, why the concern that he was going to publish it again in the *Washington Historical Quarterly* in 1931? But Rich wrote, "When your history is published." Is Rich referring to the *History of King County, Washington*? Yet, in the same sentence he refers to "your copy to appear in the 'Quarterly.'" Is he referring to this thirty-two-page history of Seathl and his daughter, Angeline, in the *Washington Historical Quarterly*? One explanation is that Bagley wrote the *Quarterly* article earlier than the 1929 book and delayed the publication of it until 1931. This would explain the confusion in chronology, but there is no evidence to confirm this. The only answer is that Rich did not write the letter in 1930. He wrote it before Bagley published his book.

In an undated letter to Bagley that is clearly after the "[1930?]" letter Rich wrote that

> I have your gracious letter of Sep 27 - Explanations not needed among friends and I trust you will call often and - very soon. . . . *Of course you would have found the speech by your able and diligent research,* [emphasis added] but it seems that previous to this time *it has been entirely overlooked since its publication 43 years ago*[240] [emphasis added] so perhaps I'm not absurd in "thinking it might for another 40 years! . . . The word "Absurd" is dangerous - I may be but I doubt it.
>
> I appreciate your inquiry about postponing your publication of Smith and care much more for the spirit than the fact it will appear.[241]

---

[240] This would date the letter 1930 after the [1930] letter.

[241] John M. Rich, Seattle, Washington, to Clarence B. Bagley, Seattle, Washington, 27 September [probably 1930 after the "1930?" letter], Transcript in the hand of John M. Rich, Clarence Bagley Collection, Manuscripts & University Archives Division, University of Washington, Seattle, Washington, 1. Hereafter cited in the text as Rich, Letter 27 September.

Rich appears to believe that he is the one responsible for uncovering the letter. If Bagley was aware of the speech before Rich why save these letters? Why save letters from someone who is a local dentist, not a prominent scholar, making the ridiculous claim that he found the speech you had already published the year before? Evidently, Bagley took some offense to Rich pointing out that Bagley had overlooked the speech and it could have remained hidden for "another 40 years" because Rich put "Absurd" in quotes. Why did Bagley use the word "absurd" if he had published the speech the year before Rich "discovered" it? Why does Rich reply obsequiously to Bagley with "Of course you would have found the speech"? If Bagley had found the speech first, why would Rich make such a comment? There is quite a difference between "would have found" and "did find" the speech. Obviously, he was replying to something Bagley had written. Bagley did publish the speech in 1929. Rich's statement makes no sense if Bagley was the first to find the speech. One thing is certain: Either Rich copied some of the Bagley's editing of Smith's original version or vice versa. There are too many similarities in the editing done by Bagley and Rich for it not to be the case.

Rich changed fifty percent of the sentences in the original version. Bagley changed eighty-seven percent of the sentences.

Bagley's Version: Smith's original text unedited by Bagley
[*Smith's original text before editing by Bagley*]
Bagley's additions

Youth is impulsive. When our young men grow angry at some real or imaginary wrong, and disfigure their faces with black paint, it denotes that their hearts are [*, also, are*

disfigured and turn] black − [,] **and then they are often cruel and** [*their cruelty is*] **relentless**, [*and knows no bounds,*] and our old men **and old women** are **unable** [*not able*] to restrain them. **Thus it has ever been. Thus it was when the white man first began to push out forefathers westward.** But let us hope that hostilities between **us** [*the red-man and his pale-face brother*] may never return. We would have everything to lose and nothing to gain.[242]

Rich's Version: Smith's original text unedited by Rich
[*Smith's original text before editing by Rich*]
Rich's additions
<u>Editing similar to Bagley's</u>
[Bagley's editing omitted by Rich]

<u>Youth is impulsive</u>. When our young men grow angry at some real or imaginary wrong, and disfigure their faces with black paint, **[it denotes that]** their hearts also are disfigured and turn black, and **[then]** <u>they are often cruel and</u> [*then their cruelty is*] relentless and **know** [*knows*] no bounds, and our old men **[and old women]** are <u>unable</u> [*not able*] **to restrain them.**
[243]<u>Thus it has ever been. Thus it was when the white man first</u> began to push [out] <u>our forefathers westward.</u> But let us hope that hostilities between the Red Man and his pale-face brothers **[us]** may never return. We would have everything to lose and nothing to gain. [244]

Did Rich see both Smith's version of the speech and Bagley's? He left out many of Bagley's additions. Did Bagley see both Smith's version and Rich's? The above paragraphs show that one of these men influenced the other. Regardless of who copied whom, the changes in the original speech are calculated changes by both authors.

---

[242]Bagley, "Angeline," 254-55. Dr. Smith begins a new paragraph here.
[243]Rich begins a new paragraph that was not in Smith's original text or in Bagley's text.
[244]Rich, *Challenge*, 38.

Rich's interest was not strictly one of historical scholarship. Rich wrote to Bagley saying, "the grandeur of the speech has not been emphasized."[245] The flourishes in Rich's version may have been for the purpose of "emphasizing the grandeur." He stated that he was bringing it to the attention of others to share its beauty and to preserve it for the "literary and historical value." In the preface of his booklet *Chief Seattle's Unanswered Challenge*, he wrote:

> This address is published because it reveals the nobility of the Soul of the American Indian, conceived and expressed by the great Chief Seattle so masterly that it naturally takes its place among the undying orations of history, and in the hope that it will reach all lovers of Indian lore and live even after . . .[246]

His entire introduction to the speech was patronizing, paternalistic and as Dr. William Arrowsmith said, "Rich tacked more nonsense onto Smith's version . . . [which]. . . was indeed worthless . . ."[247] In Rich's prologue he speaks of the "Mysterious Brotherhood" looking "into the horoscope of the world" and the "prophetic light revealed the dawn of a New World, showing its spiritual and material outlines reflecting the advent of the Aquarian Age."[248] Rich went on to say that Seathl was a messenger from the "Mystics."

> The power of the Mystics, though able, must not change the material destiny. But they could immortalize a little of the worth in the spirit of the passing races, [and] . . . That Spirit incarnated as the last Great Chief [Seathl] . . . to pronounce the Mighty Oration of Farewell.[249]

It is safe to assume that Rich felt responsibility to help the "Mystics" "immortalize" and pass on "the Mighty Oration of Farewell."

---

[245]Rich, Letter 27 September, 2.
[246]Rich, *Challenge*, 9.
[247]William Arrowsmith, Bristol, Vermont, to Janice Krenmayr, Seattle, 6 January 1975. The Museum of History and Industry, Seattle, Washington.
[248]Rich, *Challenge*, 7.
[249]Rich, *Challenge*, 8.

At the end of his booklet, Rich included a letter written by the law firm of Clark R. Belknap to authenticate Rich's version. A portion of the letter reads as follows:

> About a week before Vivian M. Carkeek[250] died (December 29, 1934) I [Belknap] had quite an extended conversation with him relative to the authenticity of the Address of Chief Seattle, as contained in your book. Mr. Carkeek told me that he had gone into the matter quite thoroughly with Dr. Henry A. Smith when the doctor was on his deathbed.[251]
>
> Dr. Smith told Mr. Carkeek that he had made extended notes of the address at the time it was given and from those notes he reconstructed the entire address. He further stated that the manuscript shown to him by Mr. Carkeek was correct.
>
> Mr. Carkeek told me that me he had compared your copy of the speech with the one approved by Dr. Smith and that they were identical. . . . [252]

This letter raises far more questions than it answers. What manuscript was "approved by Dr. Smith" and then compared to Rich's version? The original speech published in the *Seattle Sunday Star* is on record and it is not identical to Rich's version. Also, Dr. Smith said he took "extended notes" and "reconstructed the entire address." In the *Seattle Sunday Star* in 1887, he wrote, "The above is but a *fragment*

---

[250]Vivian Carkeek was a wealthy capitalist, a mover and shaker in Seattle at this time. Rick Caldwell, interview by the author, 1 November 1996, Sebastopol, California, telephone.

[251]In 1956 C.T. Conover, a columnist for the *Seattle Times*, wrote to Dr. Smith's daughter, Mrs. C. F. Graff, asking about Dr. Smith. She wrote, that "In 1892 he suffered a fractured skull and internal injuries. He had to trust his business affairs to others and experienced severe losses. . . . In 1915, while working in his garden he was thoroughly drenched in a sudden downpour and got a severe cold from which he never rallied. He died peacefully in a coma August 14." as quoted in C.T. Conover "Just Cogitating: More Details Told of Dr. Henry Smith's Life," the *Seattle Times*, Sunday 18 November 1956, 6.

[252]Rich, *Challenge*, 45.

[emphasis added] of his speech, and lacks all the charm lent by the grace and earnestness of the sable old orator, and the occasion."[253]

During the early part of the 20th century, a number of vanity history books or "mug books" were published on the Puget Sound pioneers and the history of the early settlement of the Sound. People often paid to have their personal histories included in these books. Many of the stories and personal histories were almost identical in these "mug books" although different authors wrote them. They gave no sources for the stories and histories. Without sources, it is hard to know whether the pioneers wrote their own personal histories, paid to have the authors include them in the "mug books" or if the authors wrote the personal histories themselves. One thing is for certain, but for a few additions and omissions they are identical. The following are examples of the personal history of Dr. Henry A. Smith from two different "vanity books":

He was a man of wonderful endurance . . .[254]

He was a man of wonderful physical endurance . . .[255]

He traveled with a large company and fortunately took with him a large supply of medicine which proved of the greatest benefit, for it was the year of the cholera scourge when so many suffered from the dread disease. Dr. Smith was instrumental in relieving the suffering and saved the lives of many during the journey.[256]

He traveled with a large company and fortunately took with him a big supply of medicine, which came into good play, for it was the year of the cholera scourge when so many emigrants suffered from the dread disease. Dr. Smith was instrumental in saving lives of so

---

[253]Smith, *Seattle Star*, 7.

[254]Herbert Hunt and Floyd C. Kaylor. Washington, *West of the Cascades: Historical and Description: The Indian, Pioneer, The Modern* (Chicago: S.J. Clarke Co., 1917), 307. Hereafter cited in the text as Hunt, *West of the Cascades*.

[255]Bagley, *History of Seattle*, 264.

[256]Hunt, *West of the Cascades*, 307.

many and also made considerable money by the exercise of his professional skill.[257]

Both authors were obviously using similar texts and making only slight changes. Is there an original they were both copying and adulterating or was one author simply following the other? Without the sources, it cannot answered. The issue of authenticity of the "mug books" is important because if this type of scholarship was an accepted practice, it may account for the liberty both Rich and Bagley took in adulterating and copying the speech. Through the years many authors have been guilty of taking the same liberties in editing Seathl's speech as Bagley and Rich. There also appears to be a pattern in the timing of the reprinting by various authors. A crisis or a period of turmoil faced America during the publication of many of these reprints

The pattern begins with Smith in 1887 with the ending of the reign of Seattle's governing elite and the pattern continues with the reprinting in 1929, 1931 and 1932, then again in 1943 and 1964. David Buerge points out that each writer has looked towards Seathl's speech as a possible solution for the crisis of the time.

> To a people confronting disturbing and oftentimes catastrophic change toward the end of the nineteenth century and the beginning of twentieth century, these words tingled with meaning. The speech appeared in histories of the city and the region, and every time a new crisis loomed, the speech and the speaker were re-examined.[258]

When Bagley, Rich and Watt reprinted Seathl's speech it was the beginning of the Great Depression. Eva Greensplit Anderson, a Puget Sound author, published a biography of Seathl written for teenagers in 1943 that portrayed Seathl as a type of pacifist.[259] In 1964

---

[257]Bagley, *History of Seattle*, 265.
[258]Buerge, "Seattle's King Arthur," 29.
[259] Ibid. It is important to remember that although World War II was often considered a "peoples' war" there was in fact dissension at home. "During the war, there were fourteen thousand strikes, involving 6,770,000 workers, more than in any comparable period in American history. In 1944 alone, a million workers were on strike, . . . strikes continued in record number-- 3 million on strike in the first half of 1946. . . . Out of 10 million drafted . . . only 43,00 refused to fight. But this was three

83

at the Second Vatican Council a "Catholic writer, Leo Metcalf, attempted to present Seattle as a Catholic lay leader."[260] None of these reprintings captured widespread attention. Even the introduction of Seathl's speech at the Vatican garnered little attention. It was not until William Arrowsmith translated it in 1969 and Ted Perry adapted the translation for a movie script in 1970 that it became known internationally. At this time once again the United States was in a crisis.

Before the late 1960s, the majority of Americans did not consider the Native Americans as "Wisdomkeepers"[261] To most Americans only progress and American ingenuity could solve the problems faced by United States. The primitive cultures of the Native Americans did not have the answers. This may be the reason the speech only remained a part of Puget Sound lore and never received national attention. There is a direct connection between the speed in which the environmental version spread worldwide and the planetary ecological crisis of the 1960's and 70's. During this same period Western cultures began redefining the image of the indigenous peoples of the world. The environmental movement held the indigenous peoples up as examples of the first ecologists. As the late Lakota Chief Matthew King said to authors Steve Wall and Harvey Arden, "It's time Indians tell the world what we know . . . about nature and about God. So I'm going to tell you what I know and who I am. You guys better listen. You got a lot to learn."[262]

One hundred three years earlier when Dr. Smith published Seathl's speech, the image of the Native Americans was quite different. The great Lakota (Sioux) warrior Crazy Horse had been dead for ten years. Sitting Bull was still alive as were most of the warriors who defeated General Custer and his men. The dominant image of the Indian was that of a savage warrior. The nation was in the midst of the Industrial Age and nature and her resources were merely another commodity to exploit. The Native Americans had been an impediment to progress for three hundred years. Not only did they not have the

<hr>

times the proportion of C.O.'s . . . in World War I. Of every six men in federal prison, one was there as a C.O. . . . The government lists about 350,000 cases of draft evasion, . . ." Zinn, Peoples' History, 408-9.

[260]Ibid.

[261]The partial title of a book; Steve Wall and Harvey Arden, *Wisdomkeepers: Meetings With Native Americans Spiritual Elders* (Hillsboro, Oregon: Beyond Words Publishing Co., 1990). Hereinafter cited in the text as Wall and Arden, *Wisdomkeepers*.

[262]Wall and Arden, *Wisdomkeepers*, 29.

solutions, they were the problem. Smith used the speech as a metaphor for the cycles of humans. Here was a great people, who thought of their existence as eternal and now found themselves on the edge of extinction. And Smith implied that the newly elected city government of Seattle would also suffer a similar demise.

Rich published his version in 1932 during the Great Depression. Bagley's first publication of the speech was before the Crash of 1929, but in 1931 he published an article on Chief Seathl and his daughter, Angeline, which included Seathl's speech. Rich stated that his purpose in publishing the speech was to preserve its grandeur and historical value for future generations. But his historical account of the speech and his attempt to put it in perspective was inaccurate, simplistic and sentimental. Rich wrote of the injustices suffered by the Native Americans and hoped that this oration would prove their nobility. Bagley on the other hand merely updated his first printing of the history of Seattle by including the speech and adding an introductory paragraph:

> Among the contributions of Dr. Henry A. Smith to the press of Washington were many valuable historical reminiscences. Among the most interesting of these was published in the *Seattle Sunday Star* of October 29, 1887, which is here reproduced both of its interest to the citizens of Seattle and because of its historical value.[263]

Clearly he included the speech for its historical significance.

Clarence Bagley and Frederic Grant's purpose may have been strictly historical. However, more often than not the speech appears to have been published during times of local or national crisis. John Rich printed the speech during the Great Depression. Eva Greensplit wrote her book in the midst of World War II. Vernon Metcalf's desire to have the Vatican recognize Seathl as a "Catholic lay leader" was in 1964 when the turmoil of the Civil Rights Movement, Vietnam War and a cultural revolution was threatening to explode. [264] Dr. William Arrowsmith and Dr. Ted Perry were working on Seathl's speech as the

---

[263]Bagley, *History of King County*, 112.
[264]Rachael Carlson's book *Silent Spring* introduced the idea that an environmental catastrophe was fast approaching if we continued our present path.

destruction of the environment was beginning to alarm the general public. It was the work of Arrowsmith and a year later Perry that crafted the famous prophetic environmental message that Chief Seathl is said to have spoken in 1854.

Chapter VI

The History of the Environmental Version

In 1969 the speech was dramatically reworked, and became the environmental speech/letter Seathl purportedly spoke.[265] Professor William Arrowsmith, at the time a professor of Classical Literature at the University of Texas, was writing on education at the Batelle Memorial Institute in Seattle in the late 1960s. While there, he picked up a collection of essays the president of Washington State University had recently published. At the end of one of the essays, there were some quotes from Smith's version of Seathl's speech. Arrowsmith said it read like prose from the Greek poet, Pindar. With interest aroused, he found the original speech. After reading it, he decided to try rewriting the speech removing the Victorian influences. Arrowsmith attempted to get a sense of how Seathl may have spoken and establish some "likely perimeters of the language." He turned to the elders of the local tribes who were the traditionalists.[266] This is the birth of Version Two of the speech. In this version there are no references to the environment or the love God has for his "red children." Those came later.

In 1970, Ted Perry, an associate professor of Theatre Arts at the University of Texas and a personal friend of Arrowsmith, heard him read Version Two of Chief Seathl's speech at an Earth Day rally. Arrowsmith's version impressed Perry. At the time, Professor Perry

---

[265]For a more detailed discussion of this matter see Appendix 6.

[266]Arrowsmith did not tell the author who he specifically talked to or which tribes he spoke to and the author failed to ask him. Seathl's great granddaughter, Dorothy Newton, was the only person Arrowsmith mentioned in any of the conversations. Arrowsmith, 1 December 1992.

had a contract with the Southern Baptist Convention to write the scripts for three films on topics of his choice. His first film dealt with pollution and the environment. He wrote:

> [I] decided that I would invent a fictitious Native American speech with more emphasis on the environment, and use it for the soundtrack of the film I was working on. . . . I mentioned to the film's producer [John Stevens] that I had been inspired by the original Chief Seattle text. I also used Chief Seattle's name in the text I wrote, which was certainly a terrible idea, although at the time it seemed innocent enough . . . . When the film, <u>Home</u>, aired on ABC-TV in 1972, I was more than surprised to find that the producer, even though we had a written contract, had taken my "written by" credit off the film, thereby promoting the text as an actual speech by Chief Seattle. When I contacted him, he said that he thought the text would sound more authentic if my name was taken off the credits and the speech was presented as that of Chief Seattle.[267]

Arrowsmith's description of what happens confirms Perry's version:

> In the early seventies a colleague at Texas [University of Texas], Ted Perry, . . . asked me if I would let him use the speech in my rendering as the basis of a filmscript. I said yes, provided I could approve of the results. Perry wrote a script - largely 'ecological' in its emphasis and freely adding new materials *ad libitum* . . . . (. . . . he had no intention of redoing Seattle and then claiming the

---

[267]After reading this Perry wrote, "I was angry and refused to do the other two films in our contract." Ted Perry to the author, 20 March 1997, Eli Gifford, Sebastopol, California. Hereafter cited in text as Perry, 20 March 1997. Ted Perry to the author, 25 October 1991, Eli Gifford, Sebastopol, California and The Seattle Museum of History and Industry, Seattle, Washington. Hereafter cited in the text as Perry, 25 October 1991. For a more detailed discussion of this matter see Appendix 7 and Appendix 8.

results were historically genuine; he was doing a script "after" Seattle's speech . . . .).

Perry tried to insist to his producer for the film (Southern Baptist Convention) that the speech was not in any sense a translation. But they overrode his decision . . . . Hence they talked glibly about a "letter" to President Pierce . . . .

In the course of their work, the Baptists added still more "material" to the speech. The bulk of *their* additions is the (Baptist) religiosity of *their* Seattle. . . . Ted Perry broke with his producer and the Baptists over their high-handed procedures.[268]

Perry's script, Version 3, is directly responsible for all the environmental statements attributed to Chief Seathl.[269] These are a few of the words Chief Seathl did not say and Perry did:

We are a part of the earth and it is a part of us. The perfumed flowers are our sisters; the deer, the horse, the great condor, these are our brothers. The rocky crests, the juices in the meadows, the body heat of the pony, and man — all belong to the same family. . . .

If we sell you the land, you must remember that it is sacred to us, and forever teach your children that it is sacred. Each ghostly reflection in the clear water of the lakes tells of events and memories in the life of my people. . . .

The earth is not his brother, but his enemy, and when he has won the struggle, he moves on. He leaves his father's graves behind, and he does not care. He kidnaps the earth from his children. And he does not care. . . .

---

[268]Parentheses are Arrowsmith's. Kaiser, "Seattle Speech(es)," 513. John Stevens said that "although Perry and I are still friends and see each other, this [film script] is a burr in our sides." Stevens, 30 April 1995.
[269]For a more detailed discussion of this matter see Appendix 7.

. . . you must remember that the air is precious to us, and our trees, and the beasts. The wind gives man his first breath and receives his last sigh. And if we sell you our land, you will keep it apart and sacred, as a place where even the white man can go to taste a wind sweetened by meadow flowers.

I have heard stories of a thousand rotting buffaloes on the prairie, left by the white men who shot them from a passing train. I do not understand. For us, the beasts are our brothers, and we kill only to stay alive. If we sell him this land, the white man must do the same, for the animals are our brothers. What is man without the beast?

Whatever befalls the earth, befalls the sons of the earth. If men spit upon the ground, they spit upon themselves. This we know. The earth does not belong to the white man, the white man belongs to the earth. This we know. All things are connected like the blood which unites our family.

The idea is strange to us. How can you buy or sell the sky, the warmth of the land, the swiftness of the antelope?

If we do not own the freshness of the air and the sparkle of the water, how can you buy them from us?

The whites too shall pass; perhaps sooner than all other tribes. Continuing to contaminate his own bed, the white man will one night suffocate in his own filth.

. . . . we do not understand what living becomes when the buffalo are all slaughtered, the wild horses all tamed, the secret corners of the forest are heavy with the scent of many men, and the view of the ripe hills blotted by talking wires. Where is the thicket? Gone. Where is the eagle? Gone. And what is it to say goodbye to the swift pony and the hunt? The end of living and the beginning of survival.[270]

Perry made no references to God in his version and never had Seathl referring to himself as a savage. Perry said: "The shortened version of my original text, as recorded for the narration of the film, also had at least one or two additions that I had not written and which, presumably, were added by the film's producers. . . . Anything added in the final version of the film was added by them."[271] John Stevens, the producer for the film, was working for Southern Baptists Radio and Television Commission at the time. Part of his job was:

> to edit film scripts and adapt them to meet the agenda and interests of the Southern Baptist Radio and Television Commission. I had edited scripts that did not have the Baptists' line dozens of times. This needed to be done so they could justify spending thousands of dollars on a film. I eventually quit my job as a producer because I got tired of shoehorning those interests into scripts.
>
> I edited the speech to fit our needs [Baptists] more closely. There was no apple pie and motherhood and so I added the references to God and I am a savage to make the Radio and Television Commission happy.
>
> I left out both my name and Ted's name in the credits because I felt it would give the script more authenticity. Ted had told me it was adapted from a speech that Chief Seattle had spoken. I did not want to muddy the waters, I wanted to keep it purer so I left our names off the credits and wrote adapted from a speech by Chief Seattle. I thought by using the word "adapted" it would be fairly obvious that it was a not word for word transcription of Seattle's speech. I did

---

[270]The original script sent to the author by Perry. While traveling around the country and shooting on location Perry shortened his "original text of the narration to go better with the locations actually found and shot." Perry, 25 October 1991, Eli Gifford, Sebastopol, California and The Seattle Museum of History and Industry, Seattle, Washington.

[271]Perry, 25 October 1991.

credit Ted by saying the script was researched by Ted Perry. . . . When I was editing the script, the only version of the speech I saw was Ted's. It was not until years later that I read Smith's or Arrowsmith's versions.[272]

Perry said he "was told much later that the shortened version of my text, as used in the film, was sent out by the film's producers as an actual speech of Chief Seattle."[273] John Stevens said:

I did not intend for the script to be distributed. I had never seen this done to any of the scripts I had worked with. It was not distributed with my authorization. I do not know if the script that was distributed had been written or spoken by Seattle, but the credits in the movie said adapted from a speech by Chief Seattle.[274]

In August of 1984, Rick Caldwell, librarian at the Seattle Museum of History and Industry, received a letter from Claude C. Cox, Director of Marketing for the Southern Baptist's Radio and Television Commission, which stated that, "18,000 people received a poster with the speech on it" in the Baptists' promotion of the movie *Home*. "We offered the poster free to all viewers writing in. Our print run indicates 2 printings, one for 10mm and a re-run of 8mm."[275]

The first publication of the environmental version was in the November 11, 1972 issue of the *Environmental Action* magazine; this was the same year that the movie *Home* was shown.[276] By this time, it was no longer a speech but a "letter written in 1855 . . . to President Pierce by Chief Sealth of the Duwamish tribe of the State of Washington."[277] In 1974 journalist Janice Krenmayr appears to have been the first to

---

[272] Stevens, 30 April 1995.

[273] Perry, 25 October 1991. For a more detailed discussion of this matter see Appendix 7, and Appendix 8.

[274] Stevens, 30 April 1995.

[275] Claude C. Cox, Fort Worth, Texas, to Rick Caldwell, Seattle, 20 August 1984, Transcript at the Museum of History and Industry, Seattle, Washington. Hereafter cited in the text as 20 August 1984.

[276] For a more detailed discussion of this matter see Appendix 9.

[277] "This earth is sacred," *Environmental Action*, 11 November 1972, 7.

notice not only the differences in tone and message between this "letter" and the original speech, but to investigate the authenticity of the "letter" and do a comparative analysis of the speech and the "letter."

Although Krenmayr was unable to make the leap from the "letter" to Perry, she was able to track down the first people to publish it and to interview Arrowsmith.[278] Shortly before her interview in April 1974 with Arrowsmith, an article entitled "The Decidedly Unforked Message of Chief Seattle," appeared in the April 1974 issue of Northwest Airlines magazine *Passages.* The article's sidebar stated the "letter" was "An adaptation of his [Seathl's] remarks, based on an English translation by William Arrowsmith."[279] Krenmayr wrote after interviewing him, "Arrowsmith, understandably, was still simmering with the questionable tribute."[280] The first time Arrowsmith saw the article was on a flight to Alaska on Northwest Airlines. When he picked up *Passages* and read the article he was so furious he rang the buzzer for the stewardess and demanded to know how they could print such garbage. He said the poor stewardess did not know what to say in the face of his fury.[281] Krenmayr picked up Arrowsmith up at the Seattle airport after his return flight from Alaska and interviewed him over lunch. By this time, he knew that its origin was Ted Perry's script, but refused to divulge this information because: "Ted Perry was a personal friend of mine and I did not want to involve him in this mess. I hadn't received the original script he sent me, but I believed him when he said 'the letter' was not the script he wrote."[282] This answers a

---

[278]Krenmayr believes it was the research librarian that "uncovered" Arrowsmith by accident. While researching the authenticity they were referring to experts in the field of translations of Indian speeches and came across Arrowsmith's name. After contacting him they found out he was coming to Seattle and that he had translated Smith's version. Krenmayr, "The earth,".

[279]"The Decidedly Unforked Message of Chief Seattle," *Passages,* April 1974, 19. Hereafter cited in the text as "Unforked Message," *Passages.*

[280]Krenmayr, "The earth," 6.

[281] Professor William Arrowsmith, interview by the author, 18 December 1991, Sebastopol, California, telephone. Hereafter cited in the text as Arrowsmith, 18 December 1991. In a letter to D. Ann Carver, Jean Arrowsmith (Arrowsmith's wife), wrote, "Ironically, Mr. Arrowsmith is flying to Alaska tomorrow, via Northwest. I hope he doesn't find the magazine. It would ruin his trip." Jean Arrowsmith, Lincoln, Vermont, to D. Ann Carver, Seattle, 29 April 1974, Transcript in the hand of Jean Arrowsmith, The Seattle Museum of History and Industry, Seattle, Washington.

[282]Arrowsmith, 18 December 1991.

question many researchers have asked: why did he not tell Krenmayr about Perry? Two months later he involved Perry "in this mess." In a letter dated 30 July 1974 to Jane Pryor, head librarian of the Washington Room at Washington State's Capitol library, Arrowsmith wrote:

> I can assert categorically the following facts:
> 1. I did not authorize the adaptation by Ted Perry (I did give him permission to use the speech as the basis of a filmscript, but I never saw the final version and would under no circumstances have approved it or permitted it to be ascribed to Seattle). . . .
> 2. The Baptists further revised Perry's version without his consent, and then expunged his fictional adaptation from record by listing him as having "researched" the material in the film credits. . . .
>
> . . . right now I want to see this abominable speech aborted as swiftly as possible.[283]

This proves beyond a doubt that by this time Arrowsmith was well aware of the origins and history behind the environmental version. In Arrowsmith's interview with Krenmayr he "never alluded to Perry [and] never spoke of any doubts as to the authenticity of Smith's version."[284] The fact that Arrowsmith did not tell Krenmayr about Perry also explains why she was unable to find the missing link between the letter and Arrowsmith's translation. But what of this letter Arrowsmith sent to Pryor? He was writing her to get any information he could on the "degree to which the Baptist version has been circulated" so he could sue the Baptist Radio and Television Commission. Was she the only one to whom Arrowsmith confided?[285]

---

[283]William Arrowsmith, Lincoln, Vermont, to Ms. Pryor, 30 July 1974, Washington Room, Washington State Capitol Library, Olympia, Washington. Hereafter cited in the text as Pryor, 30 July 1974.

[284]Janice Krenmayr, interview by author, 11 November 1996, Sebastopol, California. Hereafter cited in the text as Krenmayr, November 1996.

[285]Pryor, 30 July 1974.

Krenmayr said that she "never spoke with Nancy Pryor and was unaware of the "July 30 letter" from Arrowsmith.[286]

Krenmayr first became aware of Seathl's "letter" when her brother, Kenneth G. Weekel, sent her an "excerpt in *Wildlife Omnibus*, a newsletter published by the National Wildlife Federation in November 15, 1973."[287] She asked for a copy of the "letter" and the editor told her "it had been 'picked up' from the *Environmental Action* magazine." The editors of the *Environmental Action* said their source had been the Seattle office of Friends of the Earth. At this point she hit a dead end because they did not know its origin or its authenticity.[288] In January 5, 1975, she wrote an article in the *Seattle Times Sunday Magazine* outlining what she and the research librarian at the *Times* had discovered.

It was Rudolph Kaiser, a University professor in Germany,[289] who finally discovered the missing link between the "letter," Ted Perry and William Arrowsmith. Sometime in the mid-1970s Kaiser became interested in investigating the authenticity of "Chief Seathl's letter" and subsequently wrote an essay in 1987 detailing his discoveries. Dale Jones, who was the Northwest Representative of Friends of the Earth wrote Kaiser:

> I first saw the letter [Version Three] in September 1972 in a now out of business Native American tabloid newspaper. . . . I clipped the article and mailed it to a few friends. Soon thereafter, the letter appeared in *Environmental Action* [November 11, 1972] and has subsequently appeared in a number of publications around the world.[290]

The lead ends here but it can be assumed that it was the Baptists' attempt to promote their movie by sending those 18,000 posters that began the legacy of the now famous "Seathl letter." When Claude Cox of the Southern Baptist's Radio and Television Commission, wrote to

---

[286]Ibid.

[287]Krenmayr, November 1996. For a more detailed discussion of this matter see Appendix 9.

[288]Krenmayr, "The earth," 6.

[289]Wissenschaftliche Hochschule des Landes Niedersaachsen, Postfach, Germany.

[290]Dale Jones of the Northwest Chapter of the Friends of the Earth, 8 July 1983 in reply to an inquiry of Kaiser quoted in Kaiser, "Seattle Speech(es)," 513.

Rick Caldwell, he said he could not help in locating the adulterated script or any research notes because the writer had "expired . . . [and] the writer's daughter and heir . . . informed us that she destroyed most of her father's files several years ago."[291] The "expired writer" was Ted Perry who is alive and well at the time of this publication.

Kaiser corresponded with Arrowsmith a number of times as he tried to track down the origin of the "letter." John Stevens, the Baptists' producer, wrote this author that "The only part of your manuscript with which I had difficulty" was the letter Arrowsmith wrote to Kaiser:[292]

> Ted Perry, . . . asked me if I would let him use the speech in my rendering as the basis of a filmscript. I said yes, provided I could approve of the results. . . .(. . . . he had no intention of redoing Seattle and then claiming the results were historically genuine; he was doing a script "after" Seattle's speech . . . .)

> Perry tried to insist to his producer for the film (Southern Baptist Convention) that the speech was not in any sense a translation. But they overrode his decision . . . . Hence they talked glibly about a "letter" to President Pierce . . . [293]

Stevens wrote that he would never have agreed to a script that had "any kind of stipulation or proviso that promised Arrowsmith could 'approve of the results,' . . . I was, after all paying for the script; it belonged to the Baptists to alter, use, throw away, whatever they deemed fit. This is understood by even the most novice freelance writer."[294] Arrowsmith, on the other hand, thought differently. There was to be no redoing of the speech. "Well, guess what. That's precisely

---

[291]Cox, 20 August 1984; Arrowsmith, 18 December 1991.
[292]John Stevens, Fort Worth, Texas, to Eli Gifford, 17 March 1997, Eli Gifford Sebastopol, California. Hereafter cited in the text as Stevens, 17 March 1997.
[293]Kaiser, "Seattle Speech(es)," 513. John Stevens said: "although Perry and I are still friends and see each other, this [film script] is a burr in our sides." Stevens, 30 April 1995.
[294]Ibid.

what I [Stevens] did with the script."[295] Arrowsmith's accusation that saying it was a letter particularly angered Stevens:

> This statement gives fresh meaning to the term, 'Bullshit.' The producer of the film (Me) never in any way, shape or form referred to the script as a translation, never mentioned President Pierce, ever at any time. The script plainly states, 'Adapted from a speech by Chief Seattle. . . ' and nothing anyone wants to believe or is desperate to believe or is determined to believe, is going to change that.[296]

The vast majority of reprints of this famous "letter" or "speech" or "address" or "message" use as a reference the article in *Passages*.[297] The author remains anonymous, but nevertheless this began the truly cynical adulterating of the text. The author was well aware of the various versions because they used both Arrowsmith and the Southern Baptists' script as its source. At the very end it states, "Excerpted from a documentary film production of the Southern Baptist Convention's Radio and Television Commission." [298] Arrowsmith's version and the movie script are hardly similar.

Arrowsmith's text:

> *Your God loves your people and hates mine* [emphasis added]. He puts his strong arm around the white man and leads him by the hand, as a father leads his little boy. He has abandoned his red children . . . No, the white man's God cannot love his red children or he would protect them. Now we are orphans. There is no one to help us.[299]

Home, movie script:

---

[295]Stevens, 17 March 1997.
[296]Ibid.
[297]For a more detailed discussion of this matter see Appendix 12.
[298]"Message," *Passages*, 20.
[299]Kaiser, Seattle Speech(es)," 522-3.

Even the white man, whose God walks and talks with him as friend to friend, cannot be exempt from the common destiny. We may be brothers after all; we shall see. One thing we know, which the white man may one day discover -- our God is the same God. *You may think now that you own him as you wish to own our land; but you cannot. He is the God of man, and His compassion is equal for the red man and the white* [emphasis added]. This earth is precious to Him, and to harm the earth is to heap contempt on its Creator. The whites too shall pass; perhaps sooner than all other tribes. Continue to contaminate your bed, and you will one night suffocate in your waste. [300]

Note how different the tone, emotion and thoughts are about God's attitude towards the whites and Native Americans.

Arrowsmith's text:

So how can we be brothers? How can your father be our father, and make us prosper and send us dreams of future greatness? *Your God is prejudiced* [author's emphasis]. He came to the white man. *We never saw him, never even heard his voice.* [author's emphasis]. He gave the white man laws, but he had no word for his red children whose numbers once filled this land as the stars filled the sky.[301]

Home, movie script:

One thing we know. *Our God is the same God* [author's emphasis]. This earth is precious to Him. Even the white man cannot be exempt from the common destiny. We may be brothers after all. We shall see.[302]

---

[300]Stevens, *Home*, 4.
[301]Kaiser, Seattle Speech(es)," 522-3.
[302]Stevens, *Home*, 4.

Obviously, there is a difference of opinion as to what Seathl said. It would be rather hard to compare these two portions and call them similar. It has to be one or the other and the author of "The Decidedly Unforked Message of Chief Seattle" choose the *Home's* version:

> We may be brothers after all; we shall see. One thing we know, which the white man may one day discover - our God is the same God. You may think now that you own Him as you wish to own our land; but you cannot. He is the God of man, and His compassion is equal for the red man and the white . . . .
>
> And with all your strength, with all your mind, with all your heart, preserve it for your children, and love it . . . . as God loves us all.
> One thing we know. Our God is the same God. This earth is precious to Him. Even the white man cannot be exempt from the common destiny. We may be brothers after all. We shall see.[303]

With the exception of Frederic Grant's reprint of Dr. Smith's transcription in 1891, Professor Arrowsmith's attempt at translating Victorian prose to prose closer to Seathl's syntax and Professor Perry's inventing of a 'fictitious Native American speech'[304] the other authors have used the speech to further their own ideas and interests, with no intent to report with historical accuracy Seathl's speech. John Stevens acknowledges his role was to adapt the speech "to meet the agenda and interests of the Southern Baptists Radio and Television Commission" so they could justify producing it to their Baptist audience.[305] Even now, people who know that this environmental speech is fraudulent continue to print it.

---

[303]"Message," *Passages*, 20.
[304]Perry, 25 October 1991.
[305]Stevens, 30 April 1995.

Chapter VII

Conclusion

The environmental version seems to be the phoenix perpetually rising from its ashes. Picture Ted Perry sitting in his church during a special youth program, one of the youths recites the environmental version, believing it to be the words of Chief Seathl. "Perry looked down in resignation. 'I'm going to be dogged by this for the rest of my life,' he thought."[306] A few years later Susan Jeffers illustrated and helped edit a children's book titled *Brother Eagle, Sister Sky: A Message from Chief Seattle*. She used the environmental version as the text for her book. Dial Books published it and the associate publisher, Skip Skwarek, claimed that "we don't have access to [Seathl's] actual words. . . ."[307] Skwarek went on to say ". . . *our feeling* [emphasis added] is that there is an indication Seattle did have these same concerns. . . . We don't know what was spoken and we feel the book captures the spirit

---

[306]Mary Murray, "The Little Green Lie," *Reader's Digest*, July 1993, 103. Hereafter cited in the text as Murray, "Green Lie." Ted Perry told the author the article written by Murray was accurate. Ted Perry interview by author, 22 March 1995, Sebastopol, California, telephone. In a letter to the author Perry also confirmed his church story, Ted Perry, Middlebury, Vermont, to Eli Gifford, Sebastopol, California, 6 November 1993, Eli Gifford, Sebastopol, California and The Museum of History and Industry Seattle, Washington.

[307] Strauss, "Mind."

All of the quotes attributed to Dial Publishers and Susan Jeffers have been read by Dial Publishers and a copy sent to Susan Jeffers. After repeated phone calls and faxes to Dial they finally said they had no comment. Vicki Kuehner, secretary of Phyllis Fogelman associate publisher at Penguin USA, interview by author, 7 January 1997, Sebastopol, California.

of what Seattle spoke that day."[308] Since there is no documentation to corroborate Smith's version, the publishers used their feelings to determine authenticity of the environmental version. Except, Ted Perry is the author of this version not Seathl. Perry wrote to the publishers, not demanding royalties, but "I [Perry] asked for 'Written by Ted Perry, inspired by a text of Chief Seattle.' That's the credit asked for whenever I am approached for permission. I have never asked for nor received any payments."[309] He did not want to perpetuate the lie that the environmental version was the words of Seathl. Jeffers' lawyer wrote back, "Susan Jeffers did not violate any copyright."[310] But there is a greater issue than simply a question of copyright laws. One Native American activist, Margo Thunderbird, has decried the Euro-Americans forcing words into the mouths of Native Americans for their own agenda:[311]

> They came for our land, for what grew or could be grown on it, for the resources in it, and for our clean air and pure water. They stole these things from us, and in the taking they also stole our free ways and the best of our leaders, killed in battles or assassinated. And now, after all that, they've come for the very last of our possessions: now they want our pride, our history, our spiritual traditions. They want to rewrite and re-make these things, to claim themselves. The lies and thefts just never end.[312]

---

[308] Stephen Strauss interview by the author, 3 July 1992, Sebastopol, California, telephone. Hereafter cited in the text as Strauss, 3 July 1992.

[309] Perry, 20 March 1997.

[310] Murray, "Green Lie," 103.

[311] The Southwest Indian Foundation's 1996 Christmas Catalog advertised a sweatshirt and greeting cards that had Chief Seathl's "lyrical deeply moving speech titled 'Seattle's Lament,' and hand-scripted in the image of the famous 'End of the Trail' silhouette. A Southwest Indian Foundation exclusive!" except it is Clarence Bagley's adulterated version of the original. *1996 Christmas Catalog,* The Southwest Indian Foundation, Gallup, New Mexico.

[312] Warren Churchill, "A Little Matter of Genocide: Native American Spirtuality and New Age Hucksterism" *Bloomsbury Review,* September/October 1988, 23. Hereafter cited in the text as Churchill, "A Little Matter of Genocide."

101

Russell Means, a well-known Oglala Lakota activist, concurs with Thunderbird:

> What's at issue here is the same old question the Europeans have always posed with regard to American Indians, whether what's ours isn't somehow theirs. And, of course, they've always answered the question in the affirmative. When they wanted our land they just announced they had a right to it and therefore owned it. When we resisted their taking of our land, they claimed we were unreasonable and committed physical genocide upon us in order to convince us to see things their way. Now, being spiritually bankrupt themselves, they want our spirituality as well. So they're making up rationalizations to explain why they're entitled to it.[313]

When the Dial Publishers defend their book based on their feelings; when their feelings come to the conclusion that Seathl had the same concern as today's environmentalists; then as Russell Means said they are "making up rationalizations to explain why they're entitled to . . . " Seathl's speech

Jeffers continued these rationalizations when she said in the back of her book: "my aim was to portray people and artifacts from a wide array of nations because the philosophy expressed in the text is one shared by most Native Americans." The publisher went on to write "This inspired Ms. Jeffers to research the Northwest Coastal Nations, Northern Plains, Southwest Plains, and Eastern Woodland Native American tribes, all of which are represented in one or more of the paintings."[314] This only shows the ignorance of both the publisher and Ms. Jeffers. In reality, Ms. Jeffers portrayed the tribes that have captured Euro-Americans" imagination for the last 150 years and Hollywood for the last seven decades: the Plains Nations. In her book every picture of a Native American, regardless of the landscape, is in the dress of a Plains Indian. What Jeffers did, was dress the message in the "prevailing image of the Indian"--the Plains Indian complete with the leather, beadwork, war bonnet, and war paint. This does not reflect those cultures where "agriculture was most developed [and] animal

---

[313]Ibid., 24.
[314]Jeffers, *Brother Eagle*.

skins gave way to wild plants and cultivated cotton as primary materials for clothing.[315] Missing are the garments made out of cedar bark or the basket hats and head nets found in the Pacific Northwest.[316] The Plains culture, at this time, was less than 200 years old and was in extreme flux. The Plains Indians were trying to integrate rapid technological advances received from their exposure to the Euro-American technology: from the horse to metal and firearms. The Plains culture Jeffers used was based on the horse that did not arrive in the Plains until the 1720s. The famous Sioux were a Woodland culture at the time and it wasn't until the 1750's that the first bands of Sioux reached the Missouri River.[317] It was another fifty years before they were moving in force to the Black Hills. Seventy-seven years later all of the Plains Nations were on reservations.[318] Using the Plains culture to represent Native Americans and the environmental version to represent the

---

[315]Carl Waldman, *Atlas of the American Indian* (New York: Fact on File, 1985) 52.

[316]Susan Jeffers spent a tremendous amount of time illustrating her book. For her illustrations to accurately reflect the culture of Chief Seathl would be a monumental task of redoing the entire book--every page, every illustration. Obviously this is not practical, but the truth of the speech is and an explanation as to why she focused on a culture that was barely established in terms of Native American cultures needs to be addressed in her future printings.

    I have had a similar problem as Jeffers in a book I co-wrote with Michael Cook called *How Can One Sell the Air*. I was not involved with the first printing which had many errors: using Bagley's version as Smith's, inaccurate history of Perry's version and a mixture of drawings of the Plains Culture and the Pacific Northwest culture. While shopping at a bookstore, I came across the first printing and found it authored by my good friend Michael Cook. I immediately called him and he asked me to rewrite the book with him. Obviously, the text has been much easier to change than the drawings, but the publisher has promised to remove all the drawings of Plains Culture in our next printing. But the phoenix perpetually rises. With our permission, the book was published in 1996 in German with all the drawings removed. They included a photograph of Chief Seathl, but instead of using the photograph on the front cover, they used a Northern Plains Indian chief in full regalia. In 1998, with our permission, the book was published in Chinese and Dutch and again the books are filled with drawings of Plains Indians despite our request that the drawings represent the Pacific Northwest Culture. Hollywood's movies of the American West has created a universal one-sided image of the indigenous peoples of America that will not die. Eli Gifford and R. Michael Cook, ed., *How Can One Sell the Air* (Summertown, Tennessee: Book Publishing Co., 1992, reprint 2005).

[317]The powerful Cheyenne Nation of the mid-1800s was almost exterminated by the Ojibwas in the 1740s forcing them into the Great Plains. By the 1750's they had joined the Black Hills tribes.

[318]By 1877 Crazy Horse was dead. Sitting Bull and his band were living in Canada.

philosophy of Native Americans perpetuates the false image of them. But considering the fact she chose the environmental version and that her latest printing 2002 still makes no mention Ted Perry's authorship, her agenda appears to be "to rewrite and remake these things, to claim. . . . [herself]" and make up "rationalizations to explain why . . . [she is] entitled to it."[319] Even the Amazon website is perpetuating the myth with the description of the book, "'How can you buy the sky? How can you own the rain and the wind?' So begin the moving words attributed to a great American Indian chief—Chief Seattle—over 100 years ago."[320]

Jeffers wrote: "The origins of Chief Seattle's words are partly obscured by the mists of time."[321] No one disputes this. The words Seathl spoke to Governor Stevens on January 12, 1854, remain uncertain, but Jeffers used the environmental version and this version is documented. It is a film script by Ted Perry and edited by John Stevens. It is not "obscured by the mists of time." After spending "three years studying," Jeffers decided that Perry's version was much closer to what Seathl must have believed.[322] She declared, "Ted Perry can say he wrote them. I can't say that he wrote them, because I don't know. . . . When you say someone is Native American, you can make certain assumptions about what he felt to be important."[323] In an

---

[319]Churchill, "A Little Matter of Genocide," 23-24.

[320] "Description of *Brother Eagle, Sister Sky*." Amazon.com: Books. n.d. Web. 24 Nov 2015.

[321]Jeffers, *Brother Eagle*.

[322]Strauss, 3 July 1992.

[323]Murray, "Green Lie," 103.

To assume that most Native Americans were environmentalists as defined by the modern world is wrong. There are a number of "diaries and reminiscences of explorers, traders, captives, settlers, missionaries, and other first-hand observers of post-contact Indian society [that] offer incontrovertible, although qualified, evidence that this was in fact so [they were not environmentalists] . . . If given the opportunity, Indians will not hesitate to overkill wildlife if it suits their purposes." John Dunn who was an "employee of the Hudson's Bay Company and resident of the Oregon Territory described the Company's propaganda campaign to encourage regulated hunting of beaver among the natives. 'But the attempt will be easily understood to be one of extreme difficulty.'" In 1831, he watched the wholesale slaughter of a herd of caribou where only a fraction of the meat was used and the rest left to rot. Samuel Hearne mentioned time and time again in his journal that his Chippewa guides killed "far more caribou and musk ox than they can use." The problem is not that the Native American's were pioneer ecologists or that they were wholesale murderers; the

interview by *The Bloomsbury Review,* Russell Means described how ludicrous it was to make such assumption:

> The Bloomsbury Review: *Could you explain the Indian concept of Mother Earth?*
>
> Russell Means: No. I couldn't. And the reason for this is that there isn't one. What there *is* are several hundred different Indian concepts concerning Earth and its feminine characteristics. Each Indian people each Indian culture, has its own concept and traditions. . . . Oh, I'm sure that at some level or another these concepts and traditions have commonalties, but there are dramatic differences, culture by culture. The traditions and concepts of each Indian culture belong to that culture. Such things are theirs. No one appointed me to speak for them . . . It would be wrong for me to purport to have some mystical right to speak in this way . . . I chose not to make my living as a culture thief.[324]

Jeffers is not alone; the "exploitation and appropriation of Native America tradition is nothing new" and presently it stretches from New Age hucksters to the halls of academia.[325]

Although Jeffers had read other versions of the speech, she was evidently unaware of the controversy surrounding the environmental version.[326] She wrote that the "speech which has since--in a variety of

---

problem is that both sides have used "over-generalized data often interpreted out of context" rather than look at the Native Americans in a much broader sense than one extreme or the other. Calvin Martin, *Keeper of the Game: Indian-Animal Relationships and the Fur Trade* (Berkeley: University of Ca. Press, 1978), 164-166.

[324] M. Annette Jaimes, "On *'Mother Earth'* An Interview with Russell Means," *Bloomsbury Review*, September/October 1988, 26. Hereafter cited in the text as Jaimes, "Interview with Russell Means."

[325] Churchill, "A Little Matter of Genocide," 23. A few examples are Dr. Jamake Highwater (aka: J. Marks), Ruth Beebe Hill's *Hanta Yo* (dialect used is unknown to Siouxian linguistics), Lynn Andrews and her many books, "Chief Red Fox," "Nino Cochise," "Sun Bear," Hyemeyohsts Storm, David Seals to name a few. "Over the past two decades, the ranks of those queuing up to cash in on the lucre and luster of "American Indian Religious Studies" have come to include a number of "New Age" luminaries reinforced by a significant portion of the university elite." Churchill, "A Little Matter of Genocide," 23.

[326] Murray, "Green Lie," 103.

forms--served as the basis of ecological movements around the world from which *Brother Eagle, Sister Sky* is drawn." There is a version, "form," that has "served as the basis of ecological movements," but the version is a lie. Seathl never said a word of it; Ted Perry wrote it! She also tried to legitimize her gross error by writing that "Joseph Campbell adapted and brought Chief Seattle's message to a wider audience with his appearance on Bill Moyers' PBS series and the book *Power of Myth*. I too have adapted Chief Seattle's words inspired--and continue to inspire--as a most compelling truth."[327] The *Power of Myth* was produced in 1987. Professor Rudolph Kaiser had just published his essay identifying, for the first time, Ted Perry as the originator of the environmental version. The essay was among a number of essays in a relatively unknown book. Given this, it quite understandable why the information may not have reached Joseph Campbell. But Jeffers wrote the book in 1991 and the *New York Times* removed it from their non-fiction bestseller list in 1992 when an article on their front page revealed Jeffers' text was not the words of Chief Seathl. So the fact that Joseph Campbell mistook Perry's version for the real speech is irrelevant.[328] What is relevant is why perpetuate the lie? Why did she decide Ted Perry's version was closer "to what Seathl must have believed,"[329] when there is no question that Perry wrote that version?

The answer can be found in another question. Why has the speech struck a chord in so many people in the Western World? It is about myths, hopes and dreams; a different understanding, a different framework of beliefs, a different direction and focus. The ancient Platonic-Cartesian dualism "which polarized experience between mind and body, spirit and substance, time and eternity, man and nature, natural and supernatural"[330] has dominated Western thinking in both the academic, scientific and religious worlds. The dualism created a climate of thought where the Earth became a commodity to conquer and exploit. In Christianity, religious artifacts, icons or ideas became

[327] Jeffers, *Brother Eagle*.
[328] It appears that Campbell conveniently ignored the historical inaccuracies as many of us did. This is assuming he knew when trains reached the Puget Sound area and knew there were no buffalo west of the Cascades.
[329] Strauss, 3 July 1992.
[330] Lynn White Jr. *Machina Ex Deo: Essays in the Dynamism of Western Culture* (Cambridge, Massachusetts:The MIT Press, 1968), p. 14. Hereafter cited in the text as White *Machina Ex Deo*.

sacred rather than the natural world. This framework of beliefs has led to the destruction of the natural world on a scale unprecedented in human history.

Between the 16th and 19th centuries Europe went through rapid social, economic, religious, scientific and technological transformations. People were being displaced from the countryside into the cities. Wealth was being transferred from royalty to the mercantile class. The Reformation of the 1500s resulted in the northwestern European countries becoming Protestant by the 1600s, but not without civil wars, inquisitions and persecutions. The ill effects of progress were becoming evident and there were some people that yearned for an age of innocence. Even as far as back as the beginning of the sixteenth century Erasmus wrote:

> The simple people of the golden age were furnished with no such school-knowledge. Nature alone sufficed to guide them; instinct, to prompt them how to live. . . . the happiest people in the world are those who are in a position to dispense artificial training altogether, and to follow solely nature as their guide. . . .[331]

A generation later, the French philosopher Michel de Montaigne voiced similar sentiments:

> It is true that the cannibals lack everything that we prize. But at least they are free from the manifold evils which we accompany our civilization, and which make our vaunted progress mockery. The whole veneer of our civilization, with all its benefits, has covered, stifled and misdirected a hundred natural activities comparable to the instinctive skill of the bird and the spider.[332]

Though Erasmus and Montaigne predated the naturalism of the Romantic Movement by centuries, "there was much talk of following nature; . . . and may be viewed as the stepping stone toward the

---

[331]Erasmus, *Praise of Folly*, 115-127, passim, quoted in Hoxie Neale Fairchild, *The Noble Savage: A Study in Romantic Naturalism* (New York: Russell & Russell, 1928), 18. Hereafter cited in the text as Fairchild, *Noble Savage*.
[332]Quoted in Fairchild, *Noble Savage*, 19.

romantic attitude."[333] For some Europeans who dreamed of a more idyllic time, the Native Americans played the role of the mythical Noble Savage.[334]

To the famous French philosopher Jean-Jaques Rousseau, the cost of progress was a "bitter price to pay."[335] The Noble Savage was a symbol for the Romantic Movement. It stood in contrast to the dark side of European civilization. With that symbol came the myth of a people who were free from the shackles of progress, who drew their virtues and morals from nature. The Noble Savage represented a people who had not been tempted by the luxurious life of Western Civilization and so had remained innocent and naive.[336] Rather than improving the natural man, civilization corrupted him. Living in nature, the Noble Savage had none of the complications of the European societies and thus, for some, was an example of the perfect human. "For the Romantics nature improved was nature destroyed."[337]

The Romantics believed the Noble Savage was a model for Europeans, but they wasted little time studying the culture of the people they mythologized.[338] What mattered was that the Native Americans played the role of the European mythical character of Adam before his fall--the Noble Savage.

For the Romantics, the Noble Savage was the symbol of a mythical time when life was simpler. Modern man has reincarnated the Noble Savage in the 20th and 21st century and named him the

---

[333]Fairchild, *Noble Savage*, 18.

[334]"The rather common restriction of the term "Noble Savage" to the American Indian has no logical basis. Negroes, South Sea Islanders, and other sorts of savages are often regarded in precisely the same light as the Redman." Fairchild, *Noble Savage*, 2.

[335]Fairchild, *Noble Savage*, 122.

[336]Obviously, many people in Western Europe did not share in the "luxurious life." But the academics, the philosophers, the segment of society who wrote, read and were affected in some way by these arguments lived the "luxurious life."

[337]Keith Thomas, *Man and the Natural World: A History of the Modern Sensibility* (New York: Pantheon Books,1983), 266. Hereafter cited in the text as Thomas, *Man and the Natural World*.

[338]"It may be added that even in the absence of any intent to deceive, the truth about savages often reached England in a rather impure state. The reports of a good many eighteenth century explorers must have been influenced by naturalistic preconceptions. And when these reports were rewritten by professional men of letters the distortion was all the greater." Fairchild, *Noble Savage*, 98.

Ecological Saint. "We are symbol-making animals. . . For we have not only a capacity for making symbols; we are under necessity to create them in order to cope humanly with our experience." [339] The Ecological Saint is a symbol for the modern man. Symbols often need stories, myths to validate the symbol and this new story is of a people whose lives and actions and relationship with the natural world were unblemished by the pollution of rational Western thought with all of its dichotomies and dualism. This myth is of a people that never existed in North America. There was greater cultural diversity among the five hundred Native American tribes than could be found at any time in Europe over the last thousand years. So it is impossible to create a myth that reflects any resemblance to the myriad of cultures living in North America.

The problem with mythologizing real people is that their reality is irrelevant to the myth. The Sioux scholar Vine Deloria Jr. wrote:

> The realities of Indian belief and existence have become so misunderstood and distorted at this point that when a real Indian stands up and speaks the truth at any given moment, he or she is not unlikely to be believed . . .[340]

In the case of Seathl, what he really said is irrelevant to the myth. People want to believe that the myth of the Ecological Saint is valid and real. "Seathl's letter" is a perfect example of the Ecological Saint myth. It speaks of compassion, love, and the sacredness of life, the brother and sisterhood that must exist among humanity. But what is more important, it prophesies the future destruction of Western man if he continues the direction Chief Seathl saw in the mid-1800s. This myth reflects the values of the late twentieth century environmentalist. It has nothing to do with a man called Seathl or his culture or the beliefs of any of the Pacific Northwest coastal tribes in the 1850s. As Margo Thunderbird said, the Euro-Americans "want to rewrite and remake these things, to claim themselves."[341] The Seathl who emerges from the historic accounts of people who knew him does not fit this model. Even Smith's image of Seathl does not fit the mold of this myth. The Seathl that emerges from the myth of the twentieth century

---

[339] *White Machina Ex Deo*, 16.
[340] Churchill, "A Little Matter of Genocide," 23.
[341] Ibid.

is rooted in our culture's recoiling from what Rousseau called the bitter price we pay for progress.

Humanity needs myths and saints. We dream of what could be. We need examples of cultures that had greater success co-existing with the natural world. But to mythologize a living people and their ancestors, to force words into the mouths of real people so that a myth can live, shows contempt and desecrates their memory, their past, and ourselves. The Suquamish Chairwoman Georgia George said, "I appreciate the environmental overtones of Perry's speech. But that doesn't excuse misrepresenting Indian leaders."[342] We need to honor Chief Seathl with the truth, not reinvent him with mythmakers. No nineteenth century Pacific Northwest Native American chief spoke the environmental version; a twentieth century Euro-American Associate Professor of Theater Arts at the University of Texas wrote them.

Perry's environmental version is an eloquent and powerful plea. It does not need a Native American to legitimize it. Chief Seathl's people considered him a great chief and during his life he was famous for his eloquence. When he spoke everyone stopped and listened to him. Mixing the environmental version of the speech and Chief Seathl's eloquence leaves only controversy and a bitter taste.

---

[342]Murray, "Green Lie," 103.

APPENDIX 1

Version 1

Recorded by Dr. Henry A. Smith[343]

1887

Old Chief Seattle was the largest Indian I ever saw, and by far the noblest looking. He stood six feet full in his moccasins, was broad shouldered, deep chested, and finely proportioned. His eyes were large, intelligent, expressive, and friendly when in repose, and faithfully mirrored the varying moods of the great soul that looked through them. He was usually solemn, silent and dignified, but on great occasions moved among assembled multitudes like a Titan among, Liliputians, and his lightest word was law.

When rising to speak in council or to tender advice, all eyes were turned upon him, and deep-toned, sonorous and eloquent sentences rolled from his lips like the ceaseless thunders of cataracts flowing from exhaustless fountains, and

HIS MAGNIFICENT BEARING

was as noble as that of the most cultivated military chieftain in command of the forces of a continent. Neither his eloquence, his dignity or grace, were acquired. They were as native to his manhood as leaves and blossoms are to a flowering almond.

His influence was marvelous. He might have been an emperor but all his instincts were democratic, and he ruled his loyal subjects with kindness and paternal benignity.

---

[343] *Seattle Sunday Star*, 29 October 1887.

He was always flattered by marked attention from white men, and never so much as when seated at their tables, and on such occasions he manifested more than anywhere else the genuine instincts of a gentleman.

When Governor Stevens first arrived in Seattle and told the natives he had been appointed commissioner of Indian affairs for Washington Territory, they gave him a demonstrative reception in front of Dr. Maynard's office, near the water front on Main street. The Bay swarmed with canoes and the shore was lined with a living mass of swaying, writhing, dusky humanity, until

OLD CHIEF SEATTLE'S

trumpet-toned voice rolled over the immense multitude, like the startling reveille of a bass drum, when silence became as instantaneous and perfect as that which follows a clap of thunder from a clear sky.

The governor was then introduced to the native multitude by Dr. Maynard, and at once commenced, in a conversational, plain and straightforward style, an explanation of his mission among them, which is too well understood to require recapitulation.

When he sat down, Chief Seattle arose with all the dignity of a senator, who carries the responsibilities of a great nation on his shoulders. Placing one hand on the governor's head, and slowly pointing heavenward with the index finger of the other, he commenced his memorable address in solemn and impressive tones.

Yonder sky that has wept tears of compassion on our fathers for centuries untold, and which, to us, looks eternal, may change. Today it is fair, tomorrow it may be overcast with clouds. My words are like the stars that never set. What Seattle says, the great chief, Washington, (*The Indians in early times thought that Washington was still alive. They knew the name to be that of a president, and when they heard of the president at Washington they mistook the name of the city for the name of the reigning chief. They thought, also, that King George was still England's monarch, because the Hudson bay traders called themselves "King George men." This innocent deception the company was shrewd enough not to explain away for the Indians had more respect for them than they would have had, had they known England was ruled by a woman. Some of us have learned better.*)[344] can rely upon, with as much certainty as our pale-face brothers can rely upon the return of the seasons.

---

[344]Dr. Smith's addition.

The son of the white chief says his father sends us greetings of friendship and good will. This is kind, for we know he has little need of our friendship in return, because his people are many. They are like the grass that covers the vast prairies, while my people are few, and resemble the scattering trees of a storm-swept plain.

The great, and I presume also good, white chief sends us word that he wants to buy our land but is willing to allow us to reserve enough to live comfortably. This indeed appears generous, for the red man no longer has rights that he need respect, and the offer may be wise, also, for we are no longer in need of a great country.

THERE WAS A TIME

when our people covered the whole land, as the waves of a wind-ruffled sea cover its shell-paved floor. But that time has long since passed away with the greatness of tribes now almost forgotten. I will not mourn over our untimely decay, nor reproach my pale-face brothers for hastening it, for we, too, may have been somewhat to blame.

When our young men grow angry at some real or imaginary wrong, and disfigure their faces with black paint, their hearts, also, are disfigured and turn black, and then their cruelty is relentless and knows no bounds, and our old men are not able to restrain them.

But let us hope that hostilities between the red-man and his pale-face brothers may never return. We would have everything to lose and nothing to gain.

True it is, that revenge, with our young braves, is considered gain, even at the cost of their own lives, but old men who stay at home in times of war, and old women, who have sons to lose, know better.

Our great father Washington, for I presume he is now our father as well as yours, since George has moved his boundaries to the north; our great and good father, I say, sends us word by his son, who, no doubt, is a great chief among his people, that if we do as he desires, he will protect us, His brave armies will be to us a bristling wall of strength, and his great ships of war will fill our harbors so that our ancient enemies far to the northward, the Simsiams and Hydas,[345] will

---

[345]The Hydas are Native Americans known as the Haidas and they lived in British Columbia on the Queen Charlotte Islands. They were also found in Alaska on the

113

no longer frighten our women and old men. Then he will be our father and we will be his children.

BUT CAN THIS EVER BE?

Your God loves your people and hates mine; he folds his strong arms lovingly around the white man and leads him as a father leads his infant son, but he has forsaken his red children; he makes your people wax strong every day, and soon they will fill the land; while my people are ebbing away like a fast-receding tide, that will never flow again. The white man's God cannot love his red children or he would protect them. They seem to be orphans and can look nowhere for help. How then can we become brothers? How can your father become our father and bring us prosperity and awaken in us dreams of returning greatness?

Your God seems to us to be partial. He came to the white man. We never saw Him; never even heard His voice; He gave the white man laws but He had no word for His red children whose teeming millions filled this vast continent as the stars fill the firmament. No, we are two distinct races and must ever remain so. There is little in common between us. The ashes of our ancestors are sacred and their final resting place is hallowed ground, while you wander away from the tombs of your fathers seemingly without regret.

Your religion was written on tables of stone by the iron finger of an angry God, lest you might forget it. The red-man could never remember nor comprehend it.

Our religion is the traditions of our ancestors, the dreams of our old men, given them by the great Spirit, and the visions of our sachems, and is written in the hearts of our people.

Your dead cease to love you and the homes of their nativity as soon as they pass the portals of the tomb. They wander far off beyond the stars, are soon forgotten, and never return. Our dead never forget the beautiful world that gave them being. They still love its winding rivers, its great mountains and its sequestered vales, and they ever yearn in tenderest affection over the lonely hearted living and often return to visit and comfort them.

---

southern portion of Prince Wales Island. The Simsiams are known as Tsimshians. They also lived around these islands and on the mainland.

Day and night cannot dwell together. The red man has ever fled the approach of the white man, as the changing mists on the mountain side flee before the blazing morning sun.

However, your proposition seems a just one, and I think my folks will accept it and will retire to the reservation you offer them, and we will dwell apart and in peace, for the words of the great white chief seem to be the voice of nature speaking to my people out of the thick darkness that is fast gathering around them like a dense fog floating inward from a midnight sea.

It matters but little where we pass the remainder of our days.

THEY ARE NOT MANY

The Indian's night promises to be dark. No bright star hovers about the horizon. Sad-voiced winds moan in the distance. Some grim Nemesis of our race is on the red man's trail, and wherever he goes he will still hear the sure approaching footsteps of the fell destroyer and prepare to meet his doom, as does the wounded doe that hears the approaching footsteps of the hunter. A few more moons, a few more winters and not one of all the mighty hosts that once filled this broad land or that now roam in fragmentary bands through these vast solitude's will remain to weep over the tombs of a people once as powerful and as hopeful as your own.

But why should we repine? Why should I murmur at the fate of my people? Tribes are made up of individuals and are no better than they. Men come and go like the waves of the sea. A tear, a tamanawus, a dirge, and they are gone from our longing eyes forever. Even the white man, whose God walked and talked with him, as friend to friend, is not exempt from the common destiny. We may be brothers after all. We shall see.

We will ponder your proposition, and when we have decided we will tell you. But should we accept it, I here and now make this first condition: That we will not be denied the privilege, without molestation, of visiting at will the graves of our ancestors and friends. Every part of this country is sacred to my people. Every hill-side, every valley, every plain and grove has been hallowed by some fond memory or some sad experience of my tribe.

EVEN THE ROCKS

that seem to lie dumb as they swelter in the sun along the silent seashore in solemn grandeur thrill with memories of past events connected with the fate of my people, and the very dust under your feet responds more lovingly to our footsteps than to yours, because it is the ashes of our ancestors, and our bare feet are conscious of the sympathetic touch, for the soil is rich with the life of our kindred.

The sable braves, and fond mothers, and glad-hearted maidens, and the little children who lived and rejoiced here, and whose very names are now forgotten, still love these solitudes, and their deep fastnesses at eventide grow shadowy with the presence of dusky spirits. And when the last red man shall have perished from the earth and his memory among white man shall have become a myth, these shores shall swarm with the invisible dead of my tribe, and when your children's children shall think themselves alone in the field, the store, the shop, upon the highway or in the silence of the woods they will not be alone. In all the earth there is no place dedicated to solitude. At night, when the streets of your cities and villages shall be silent, and you think them deserted, they will throng with the returning hosts that once filled and still love this beautiful land. The white man will never be alone. Let him be just and deal kindly with my people, for the dead are not altogether powerless.

Other speakers followed, but I took no notes. Governor Stevens' reply was brief. He merely promised to meet them in general council on some future occasion to discuss the proposed treaty. Chief Seattle's promise to adhere to the treaty, should one be ratified, was observed to the letter, for he was ever the unswerving and faithful friend of the white man. The above is but a fragment of his speech, and lacks all the charm lent by the grace and earnestness of the sable old orator, and the occasion.
[*H. A. Smith*]

APPENDIX 2

Version 1 A

Edited by Frederic Grant[346]

1891

Old Chief Seattle was the largest Indian I ever saw, and by far the noblest looking. He stood nearly six feet in his moccasins, was broad shouldered, deep chested, and finely proportioned. His eyes were large, intelligent, expressive, and friendly when in repose, and faithfully mirrored the varying moods of the great soul that looked through them. He was usually solemn, silent and dignified, but on great occasions moved among assembled multitudes like a Titan among, Lilliputians, and his lightest word was law.

When rising to speak in council or to tender advice, all eyes were turned upon him, and deep-toned, sonorous and eloquent sentences rolled from his lips like the ceaseless thunders of cataracts flowing from exhaustless fountains, and his magnificent bearing was as noble as that of the most cultivated military chieftain in command of the forces of a continent. Neither his eloquence, his dignity or grace was acquired. They were as native to his manhood as leaves and blossoms are to a flowering almond.

His influence was marvelous. He might have been an emperor but all his instincts were democratic, and he ruled his loyal subjects with kindness and paternal benignity.

He was always flattered by marked attention from white men, and never so much as when seated at their tables, and on such occasions he manifested more than anywhere else the genuine instincts of a gentleman.

---

[346]*History of Seattle, Washington; With Illustrations and Biographical Sketches of Some of Its Prominent Men and Pioneers* (New York: American Publishing and Engraving Company, 1891).

117

When Governor Stevens first arrived in Seattle and told the natives that he had been appointed Commissioner of Indian affairs for Washington Territory, they gave him a demonstrative reception in front of Dr. Maynard's office, near the water front on Main Street. The Bay swarmed with canoes and the shore was lined with a living mass of swaying, writhing, dusky humanity, until old Chief Seattle's trumpet-toned voice rolled over the immense multitude, like the startling reveille of a bass drum, when silence became as instantaneous and perfect as that which follows a clap of thunder from a clear sky.

The Governor was then introduced to the native multitude by Dr. Maynard, and at once commenced, in a conversational, plain and straightforward style, an explanation of his mission among them, which is too well understood to require recapitulation.

When he sat down, Chief Seattle arose, with all the dignity of a senator, who carries the responsibilities of a great nation on his shoulders. Placing one hand on the Governor's head, and slowly pointing heavenward with the index finger of the other, he commenced his memorable address in solemn and impressive tones:

Yonder sky has wept tears of compassion on our fathers for centuries untold, and which, to us, looks eternal, may change. To-day it is fair, to-morrow it may be overcast with clouds. My words are like stars that never set. What Seattle says, the great chief, Washington, (*the Indians in early times thought that Washington was still alive. They knew the name to be that of a president, and when they heard of the president at Washington they mistook the name of the city for the name of the reigning chief. They thought, also, that King George was still England's monarch, because the Hudson bay traders called themselves "King George men." This innocent deception the company was shrewd enough not to explain away for the Indians had more respect for them than they would have had, had they known England was ruled by a woman. Some of us have learned better.*)[347] can rely upon, with as much certainty as our pale-face brothers can rely upon the return of the seasons.[348] The son of the white chief says his father sends us greetings of friendship and good-will. This is kind, for we know he has little need of our friendship in return, because his people are many. They are like the grass that covers the vast prairies, while my people are few, and resemble the scattering trees of a storm-swept plain.

The great, and I presume also good, white chief sends us word that he wants to buy our land but is willing to allow us to reserve

---

[347]Dr. Smith's addition.
[348]Dr. Smith begins a new paragraph here.

enough to live comfortably. This indeed appears generous, for the red man no longer has rights that he need respect, and the offer may be wise, also, for we are no longer in need of a great country.[349] There was a time when our people covered the whole land as the waves of a wind-ruffled sea cover its shell-paved floor. But that time has long since passed away with the greatness of tribes now almost forgotten. I will not mourn over our untimely decay, nor reproach my pale-face brothers with hastening it, for we, too, may have been somewhat to blame.

When our young men grow angry at some real or imaginary wrong and disfigure their faces with black paint, their hearts, also, are disfigured and turn black, and then their cruelty is relentless and knows no bounds, and our old men are not able to restrain them.

But let us hope that hostilities between the red man and his pale face brothers may never return. We would have everything to lose and nothing to gain.

True it is that revenge, with our young braves, is considered gain, even at the cost of their own lives, but old men who stay at home in times of war, and old women who have sons to lose, know better.

Our great father Washington, for I presume he is now our father as well as yours, since George has moved his boundaries to the north; our great and good father, I say, sends us word by his son, who, no doubt, is a great chief among his people, that if we do as he desires, he will protect us, His brave armies will be to us a bristling wall of strength, and his great ships of war will fill our harbors so that our ancient enemies far to the northward, the Simsiams and Hydas, will no longer frighten our women and old men. Then he will be our father and we will be his children.[350] But can that ever be? Your God loves your people and hates mine; he folds his strong arms lovingly around the white man and leads him as a father leads his infant son, but he has forsaken his red children; he makes your people wax strong every day, and soon they will fill the land; while our people are ebbing away like a fast-receding tide, that will never flow again. The white man's God cannot love his red children or he would protect them. They seem to be orphans and can look nowhere for help. How then can we become brothers? How can your father become our father and bring us prosperity and awaken in us dreams of returning greatness?

---

[349]Dr. Smith begins a new paragraph centering this phrase.
[350]Dr. Smith begins a new paragraph here.

Your God seems to us to be partial. He came to the white man. We never saw Him; never even heard His voice; He gave the white man laws but He had no word for His red children whose teeming millions filled this vast continent as the stars fill the firmament. No, we are two distinct races and must ever remain so. There is little in common between us. The ashes of our ancestors are sacred and their final resting place is hallowed ground, while you wander away from the tombs of your fathers seemingly without regret.

Your religion was written on tables of stone by the iron finger of an angry God, lest you might forget it. The red man could never remember nor comprehend it.

Our religion is the traditions of our ancestors, the dreams of our old men, given them by the great Spirit, and the visions of our sachems, and is written in the hearts of our people.

Your dead cease to love you and the homes of their nativity as soon as they pass the portals of the tomb. They wander far off beyond the stars, are soon forgotten and never return. Our dead never forget the beautiful world that gave them being. They still love its winding rivers, its great mountains and its sequestered vales, and they ever yearn in tenderest affection over the lonely hearted living and often return to visit and comfort them.

Day and night cannot dwell together. The red man has ever fled the approach of the white man, as the changing mists on the mountain side flee before the blazing morning sun.

However, your proposition seems a just one, and I think my folks will accept it and will retire to the reservation you offer them, and we will dwell apart and in peace, for the words of the great white chief seem to be the voice of nature speaking to my people out of the thick darkness that is fast gathering around them like a dense fog floating inward from a midnight sea.

It matters but little where we pass the remainder of our days. They are not many. The Indian's night promises to be dark. No bright star hovers about the horizon. Sad-voiced winds moan in the distance. Some grim Nemesis of our race is on the red man's trail, and wherever he goes he will still hear the sure approaching footsteps of the fell destroyer and prepare to meet his doom, as does the wounded doe that hears the approaching footsteps of the hunter. A few more moons, a few more winters and not one of all the mighty hosts that once filled this broad land or that now roam in fragmentary bands through these vast solitudes will remain to weep over the tombs of a people once as powerful and as hopeful as your own.

But why should we repine? Why should I murmur at the fate of my people? Tribes are made up of individuals and are no better than they. Men come and go like the waves of the sea. A tear, a tamanawus, a dirge, and they are gone from our longing eyes forever. Even the white man, whose God walked and talked with him, as friend to friend, is not exempt from the common destiny. We *may* [351] be brothers after all. We shall see.

We will ponder your proposition, and when we have decided we will tell you. But should we accept it, I here and now make this first condition: That we will not be denied the privilege, without molestation, of visiting at will the graves of our ancestors and friends. Every part of this country is sacred to my people. Every hillside, every valley, every plain and grove has been hallowed by some fond memory or some sad experience of my tribe. Even the rocks that seem to lie dumb as they swelter in the sun along the silent seashore in solemn grandeur thrill with memories of past events connected with the fate of my people, and the very dust under your feet responds more lovingly to our footsteps than to yours, because it is the ashes of our ancestors, and our bare feet are conscious of the sympathetic touch, for the soil is rich with the life of our kindred.

The sable braves, and fond mothers, and glad-hearted maidens, and the little children who lived and rejoiced here, and whose very names are now forgotten, still love these solitudes, and their deep fastnesses at eventide grow shadowy with the presence of dusky spirits. And when the last red man shall have perished from the earth and his memory among white man shall have become a myth, these shores shall swarm with the invisible dead of my tribe, and when your children's children shall think themselves alone in the field, the store, the shop, upon the highway or in the silence of the woods they will not be alone. In all the earth there is no place dedicated to solitude. At night, when the streets of your cities and villages shall be silent, and you think them deserted, they will throng with the returning hosts that once filled and still love this beautiful land. The white man will never be alone. Let him be just and deal kindly with my people, for the dead are not altogether powerless.

---

[351] Grant italicized this.

Other speakers followed, but I took no notes. Governor Stevens' reply was brief. He merely promised to meet them in general council on some future occasion to discuss the proposed treaty. Chief Seattle's promise to adhere to the treaty, should one be ratified, was observed to the letter, for he was ever the unswerving and faithful friend of the white man. The above is but a fragment of his speech, and lacks all the charm lent by the grace and earnestness of the sable old orator and the occasion.[352]

---

[352]Dr. Smith's addition.

APPENDIX 3

Version 1 B

Edited by Clarence B. Bagley[353]

1931

Yonder sky that has wept tears of compassion upon my people for centuries untold, and which to us appears changeless and eternal, may change. Today is fair. Tomorrow it may be overcast with clouds. My words are like stars that never change. Whatever Seattle says the great chief at Washington can rely upon with as much certainty as he can upon the return of the sun or the seasons. The White Chief says that Big Chief at Washington sends us greetings of friendship and good will. This is kind of him for we know he has little need of our friendship in return. His people are many. They are like the grass that covers the vast prairies. My people are few. They resemble the scattering trees of a storm-swept plain. The Great--and I presume--good White Chief sends us word that he wishes to buy our land but is willing to allow us enough to live comfortably. This indeed appears just, even generous for the Red Man no longer has rights that he need respect, and the offer may be wise also, as we are no longer in need of an extensive country.

There was a time when our people covered the land as the waves of a wind-ruffled sea cover its shell-paved floor, but that time long since passed away with the greatness of tribes that are now but a mournful memory. I will not dwell on, nor mourn over, our untimely

---

[353]Clarence B. Bagley, *History of King County Washington.* Vol. 1 (Chicago, Seattle: S.J. Clarke Publishing Co., 1929); "Chief Seattle and Angeline," *The Washington Historical Quarterly* Vol. 22: 1931.

decay, nor reproach my paleface brothers with hastening it as we too may have been somewhat to blame.

Youth is impulsive. When our young men grow angry at some real or imaginary wrong, and disfigure their faces with black paint, it denotes that their hearts are black--and then they are often cruel and relentless and our old men and old women are unable to restrain them. Thus it has ever been. Thus it was when the white man first began to push out forefathers westward. But let us hope that hostilities between us may never return. We would have everything to lose and nothing to gain. Revenge by young braves, is considered gain, even at the cost of their own lives, but old men who stay at home in times of war, and mothers who have sons to lose, know better.

Our good father Washington--for I presume he is now our father as well as yours, since King George has moved his boundaries further north--our great and good father, I say, sends us word that if we do as he desires he will protect us. His brave warriors will be to us a bristling wall of strength, and his wonderful ships of war will fill our harbors so that our ancient enemies far to the northward--the Hidas and Timpsions, will cease to frighten our women, children and old men. Then in reality will he be our father and we his children. But can that ever be? Your God is not our God! Your God loves your people and hates mine. He folds his strong protecting arms lovingly around the pale face and leads him by the hand him as a father leads his infant son--but He has forsaken His red children--if they are really His. Our God, the Great Spirit, seems also to have forsaken us, Your God makes your people wax strong every day. Soon they will fill all the land. Our people are ebbing away like a rapidly receding tide, that will never return. The white man's God cannot love our people or he would protect them. They seem to be orphans who can look nowhere for help. How then can we be brothers? How can your God become our God and renew our prosperity and awaken in us dreams of returning greatness. If we have a common Heavenly Father He must be partial-- for He came to His pale-face children. We never saw Him. He gave you laws but had no word for His red children whose teeming multitudes once filled this vast continent as the stars fill the firmament. No. We are two distinct races with separate origins and separate destinies. There is little in common between us.

To us the ashes of our ancestors are sacred and their resting place is hallowed ground. You wander far away from the graves of your ancestors and seemingly without regret. Your religion was written on tables of stone by the iron finger of your God so that you could not forget. The Red Man could never comprehend nor remember it. Our religion is the traditions of our ancestors--the dreams of our old men, given them in the solemn hours of the night by the Great Spirit; and visions of our sachems, and is written in the hearts of our people.

Your dead cease to love you and the land of their nativity as soon as they pass the portals of the tomb and wander away beyond the stars. They are soon forgotten and never return. Our dead never forget the beautiful world that gave them being. They still love its verdant valleys, its murmuring rivers, its magnificent mountains, sequestered vales and verdant-lined lakes and bays, and ever yearn in tender, fond affection over the lonely hearted living, and often return from the Happy Hunting Ground to visit, guide, console and comfort them.

Day and night can not dwell together. The Red Man has ever fled the approach of the White Man as the morning mists flees before the rising sun.

However, your proposition seems fair, and I think that my folks will accept it and will retire to the reservation you offer them. Then we will dwell apart in peace for the words of the Great White Chief seem to be the voice of Nature speaking to my people out of the dense darkness.

It matters little where we pass the remnant of our days. They will not be many. The Indian's night promises to be dark. Not a single star of hope hovers above his horizon. Sad-voiced winds moan in the distance. Grim Nemesis seems to be on the Red Man's trail, and wherever he goes he will hear the approaching footsteps of his fell destroyer and prepare to stolidly meet his doom, as does the wounded doe that hears the approaching footsteps of the hunter.

A few more moons. A few more winters --and not one of the descendants of the mighty hosts that once moved over this broad land or lived in happy homes, protected by the Great Spirit, will remain to mourn over the graves of a people--once more powerful and hopeful than yours. But why should I mourn at the untimely fate of my people? Tribes follow tribe, and nations follow nations, like the waves of the sea. It is the order of nature, and regret is useless. Your time of decay may be distant--but it will surely come, for even the White Man whose God walked and talked with him as friend with friend, can not be exempt from the common destiny. We may be brothers after all. We shall see.

We will ponder your proposition and when we decide we will let you know. But should we accept it, I here and now make this condition--that we will not be denied the privilege without molestation, of visiting at any time the tombs of our ancestors, friends and children. Every part of this soil is sacred, in the estimation of my people. Every hillside, every valley, every plain and grove, has been hallowed by some sad or happy event in days long vanished. Even the rocks, which seem to be dumb and dead as they swelter in the sun along the silent shore, thrill with memories of stirring events connected with the lives of my people, and the very dust upon which you now stand responds more lovingly to their footsteps than to yours, because it is rich with the dust of our ancestors and our bare feet are conscious of the sympathetic touch. Our departed braves, and fond mothers, glad, happy-hearted maidens, and even the little children who lived here and rejoiced here for a brief season, still love these somber solitudes, and at eventide they grow shadowy of returning spirits. And when the last Red Man shall have perished, and the memory of my tribe shall have become a myth among the white man, these shores shall swarm with the invisible dead of my tribe, and when your children's children shall think themselves alone in the field, the store, the shop, upon the highway, or in the silence of the pathless woods, they will not be alone. In all the earth there is no place dedicated to solitude. At night when the streets of your cities and villages are silent and you think them deserted, they will throng with the returning hosts that once filled them and still love this beautiful land. The White Man will never be alone.

Let him be just and deal kindly with my people, for the dead are not powerless. Dead--I say? There is no death. Only a change of worlds.

APPENDIX 4

Version 1C

Edited By John M. Rich[354]

1932

Old Chief Seattle was the largest Indian I ever saw, and by far the noblest looking. He stood nearly six feet in his moccasins, was broad shouldered, deep chested, and finely proportioned. His eyes were large, intelligent, expressive, and friendly when in repose, and faithfully mirrored the varying moods of the great soul that looked through them.

He was usually solemn, silent and dignified, but on great occasions moved among assembled multitudes like a Titan among, Lilliputians, and his lightest word was law.

When rising to speak in council or to tender advice, all eyes were turned upon him, and deep-toned, sonorous and eloquent sentences rolled from his lips like the ceaseless thunders of cataracts flowing from exhaustless fountains, and his magnificent bearing was as noble as that of the most civilized military chieftain in command of the forces of a continent.

Neither his eloquence, his dignity nor his grace were acquired. They were as native to his manhood as are needles and cones to a great pine tree

His influence was marvelous. He might have been an emperor but all his instincts were democratic, and he ruled his loyal subjects with kindness and paternal benignity.

He was always flattered by marked attention from white men, and never so much as when seated at their tables, and on such occasions he manifested more than anywhere else the genuine instincts of a gentleman.

---

[354] "Seattle's Unanswered Challenge" (Fairfield, Washington: Ye Galleon Press. 1932/1970), 31-41.

When Governor Stevens first arrived in Seattle and told the natives that he had been appointed Commissioner of Indian Affairs for Washington Territory, they gave him a demonstrative reception in front of Dr. Maynard's office, near the waterfront on Main Street.

The Bay swarmed with canoes and the shore was lined with a living mass of swaying, writhing, dusky humanity, until old Chief Seattle's trumpet tones voice rolled over the immense multitude, like the startling reveille of a bass drum, when silence became as instantaneous and perfect.

The Governor was then introduced by Dr. Maynard, to the native multitude and at once commenced, in a conversational, plain and straightforward style, an explanation of his mission among them, which is too well understood to require recapitulation.

When he sat down, Chief Seattle arose, with all the dignity of a senator, who carries the responsibility of a great nation upon his shoulders. Placing one hand on the Governor's head, and slowly pointing heavenward with the index finger of the other, he commenced his memorable address in solemn and impressive tones:

Yonder sky that has wept tears of compassion upon our fathers for centuries untold, and which to us looks eternal, may change. Today it is fair, tomorrow it may be overcast with clouds.

My words are like stars that never set. What Seattle says the Great Chief at Washington can rely upon with as much certainty as our paleface brothers can rely upon the return of the seasons.

The son of the White Chief says his father sends us greetings of friendship and good will. This is kind of him for we know he has little need of our friendship in return because his people are many. They are like the grass that covers the vast prairies, while my people are few; they resemble the scattering trees of a storm-swept plain.

The Great--and I presume--good, White Chief, sends us word that he wants to buy our lands but is willing to allow us to reserve enough to live on comfortably. This indeed appears generous, for the Red Man no longer has rights that he need respect, and the offer may be wise, also, for we are no longer in need of a great country.

There was a time when our people covered the whole land as the waves of a wind-ruffled sea covers its shell-paved floor, but that time has long since passed away with the greatness of tribes now almost forgotten. I will not dwell on nor mourn over our untimely decay, nor reproach my paleface brothers with hastening it, for we, too, may have been somewhat to blame.

Youth is impulsive. When our young men grow angry at some real or imaginary wrong, and disfigure their faces with black paint, their hearts also are disfigured and turn black, and then they are often cruel and relentless and know no bounds, and our old men are unable to restrain them.

Thus it has ever been. Thus it was when the white man first began to push our forefathers westward. But let us hope that the hostilities between the Red Man and his paleface brother may never return. We would have everything to lose and nothing to gain.

It is true that revenge by our young braves is considered gain, even at the cost of their own lives, but old men who stay at home in times of war, and mothers who have sons to lose, know better.

Our good father at Washington--for I presume he is now our father as well as yours, since King George has moved his boundaries farther north--our great and good father, I say, sends us word that if we do as he desires he will protect us.

His brave warriors will be to us a bristling wall of strength, and his great ships of war will fill our harbors so that our ancient enemies far to the northward--the Sinsiams, Hydas and Tsimpsians--will no longer frighten our women and old men. Then will he be our father and we his children.

But can this ever be? Your God is not our God! Your God loves your people and hates mine! He folds His strong arms lovingly around the white man and leads him as a father leads his infant son-- but He has forsaken His red children, if they are really His. Our God, the Great Spirit, seems, also, to have forsaken us. Your God makes your people wax strong every day - soon they will fill the land.

My people are ebbing away like a fast-receding tide that will never flow again. The white man's God cannot love His red children or He would protect them. We seem to be orphans who can look nowhere for help.

How, then, can we become brothers? How can your God become our God and renew our prosperity and awaken in us dreams of returning greatness?

Your God seems to us to be partial. He came to the white man. We never saw Him, never heard His voice. He gave the white man laws, but had no word for His red children whose teeming millions once filled this vast continent as the stars fill the firmament.

No, We are two distinct races and must ever remain so, with separate origins and separate destinies. There is little in common between us.

To us the ashes of our ancestors are sacred and their final resting place is hallowed ground, while you wander far from the graves of your ancestors and, seemingly, without regret.

Your religion was written on tablets of stone by the iron finger of an angry God, lest you might forget it. The Red Man could never comprehend nor remember it.

Our religion is the traditions of our ancestors - the dreams of our old men, given to them in the solemn hours of the night by the Great Spirit, and the visions of our Sachems, and is written in the hearts of our people.

Your dead cease to love you and the land of their nativity as soon as they pass the portals of the tomb--they wander far away beyond the stars, are soon forgotten and never return.

Our dead never forget this beautiful world that gave them being. They still love its winding rivers, its great mountains and its sequestered vales, and they ever yearn in tenderest affection over the lonely-hearted living, and often return to visit, guide and comfort them.

Day and night cannot dwell together. The Red Man has ever fled the approach of the white man, as the changing mists on the mountin [sic] side flees before the blazing sun.

However, your proposition seems a just one, and I think my people will accept it and will retire to the reservation you offer them. Then we will dwell apart in peace, for the words of the Great White Chief seem to be the voice of Nature speaking to my people out of the thick darkness, that is fast gathering around them like a dense fog floating inward from a midnight sea.

It matters little where we pass the remnant of our days. They are not many. The Indian's night promises to be dark. No bright star hovers above the horizon. Sad-voiced winds moan in the distance. Some grim Fate of our race is on the Red Man's trail, and wherever he goes he will still hear the sure approaching footsteps of his fell destroyer and prepare to stolidly meet his doom, as does the wounded doe that hears the approaching footsteps of the hunter.

A few more moons, a few more winters--and not one of all the mighty hosts that once filled this broad land and that now roam in fragmentary bands through these vast solitudes or lived in happy homes, protected by the Great Spirit, will remain to weep over the graves of a people once as powerful and as hopeful as your own!

But why should I repine? Why should I murmur at the fate of my people? Tribes are made up of individuals and are no better than they. Men come and go like the waves of the sea. A tear, a tamanawus, a dirge, and they are gone from our longing eyes forever. It is the order of Nature. Even the white man, whose God walked and talked with him as friend to friend, is not exempt from the common destiny. We may be brothers, after all. We shall see.

We will ponder your proposition, and when we decide we will tell you. But should we accept it, I here and now make this first condition - that we will not be denied the privilege, without molestation, of visiting at will the graves of our ancestors, friends and children.

Every part of this country is sacred to my people. Every hillside, every valley, every plain and grove has been hallowed by some fond memory or sad experience of my tribe. Even the rocks, which seem to lie dumb as they swelter in the sun along the silent sea shore in solemn grandeur thrill with memories of past events connected with the lives of my people.

The very dust under your feet responds more lovingly to our footsteps than to yours, because it is the ashes of our ancestors, and our bare feet are conscious of the sympathetic touch, for the soil is rich with the life of our kindred.

The noble braves, and fond mothers, and glad, happy-hearted maidens, and even the little children, who lived and rejoiced here, for a brief season, and whose very names are now forgotten, still love these somber solitudes and their deep fastnesses which, at eventide grow shadowy with the presence of dusky spirits.

And when the last Red Man shall have perished from the earth and his memory among the white men shall have become a myth, these shores shall swarm with the invisible dead of my tribe, and when your children's children shall think themselves alone in the fields, the store, the shop, upon the highway, or in the silence of the pathless woods they will not be alone. In all the earth there is no place dedicated to solitude.

At night, when the streets of your cities and villages will be silent and you think them deserted, they will throng with the returning hosts that once filled and still love this beautiful land.

The white man will never be alone. Let him be just and deal kindly with my people, for the dead are not powerless.

Dead--did I say? There is no death. Only a change of worlds!

The above is but a fragment of Chief Seattle's speech, and lacks all the charm lent by the grace and earnestness of the sable old orator and the occasion.[355]

---

[355]Dr. Smith's addition; Rich's editing.

APPENDIX 5

Version 1 B

Edited by Roberta Frye Watt[356]

1931

Yonder sky that has wept tears of compassion upon my people for centuries untold, and which to us appears changeless and eternal, may change. Today is fair. Tomorrow it may be overcast with clouds. My words are like stars that never change. Whatever Seattle says the great chief Washington can rely upon with as much certainty as he can rely upon the return of the sun or the seasons. The White Chief says that Big Chief at Washington sends us greetings of friendship and goodwill. This is kind of him for we know he has little need of our friendship in return. His people are many. They are like the grass that covers the vast prairies. My people are few. They resemble the scattering trees of a storm-swept plain. The great--and I presume--good White Chief sends us word that he wishes to buy our land but is willing to allow us enough to live comfortably. This indeed appears just, even generous for the Red Man no longer has rights that he need respect, and the offer may be wise also, as we are no longer in need of an extensive country.

There was a time when our people covered the land as the waves of a wind-ruffled sea cover its shell paved floor, but that time long since passed away with the greatness of tribes that are now but a mournful memory. I will not dwell on, nor mourn over, our untimely decay, nor reproach my paleface brothers with hastening it as we too may have been somewhat to blame.

---

[356]Roberta Frye Watt, *The Story of Seattle* (Portland: Binford & Mort, 1931), 179-182.

Youth is impulsive. When our young men grow angry at some real or imaginary wrong, and disfigure their faces with black paint, it denotes that their hearts are black, and that they are often cruel and relentless, and our old men and old women are unable to restrain them. Thus it has ever been. Thus it was when the white men first began to push out forefathers further westward. But let us hope that hostilities between us may never return. We would have everything to lose and nothing to gain. Revenge by young men is considered gain, even at the cost of their own lives, but old men who stay at home in times of war, and mothers who have sons to lose, know better.

Our good father Washington--for I presume he is now our father as well as yours, since King George has moved his boundaries further north--our great and good father, I say, sends us word that if we do as he desires he will protect us. His brave warriors will be to us a bristling wall of strength, and his wonderful ships of war will fill our harbors so that our ancient enemies far to the northward--the Hydas and Tsimpsians, will cease to frighten our women, children and old men. Then in reality will he be our father and we his children. But can that ever be? Your God is not our God! Your God loves your people and hates mine. He folds his strong protecting arms lovingly around the pale face and leads him by the hand him as a father leads his infant son--but He has forsaken His red children--if they are really his. Our God, the Great Spirit, seems also to have forsaken us. Your God makes your people wax strong every day. Soon they will fill all the land. Our people are ebbing away like a rapidly receding tide that will never return. The white man's God cannot love our people or He would protect them. They seem to be orphans who can look nowhere for help. How then can we be brothers? How can your God become our God and renew our prosperity and awaken in us dreams of returning greatness. If we have a common heavenly father He must be partial-- for He came to His paleface children. We never saw Him. He gave you laws but He had no word for his red children whose teeming multitudes once filled this vast continent as the stars fill the firmament. No; we are two distinct races with separate origins and separate destinies. There is little in common between us.

To us the ashes of our ancestors are sacred and their resting place is hallowed ground. You wander far away from the graves of your ancestors and seemingly without regret. Your religion was written upon tables of stone by the iron finger of your God so that you could not forget. The Red Man could never comprehend nor remember it. Our religion is the traditions of our ancestors--the dreams of our old men, given them in the solemn hours of the night by the Great Spirit; and the visions of our sachems, and is written in the hearts of our people.

Your dead cease to love you and the land of their nativity as soon as they pass the portals of the tomb and wander way beyond the stars. They are soon forgotten and never return. Our dead never forget the beautiful world that gave them being. They still love its verdant valleys, its murmuring rivers, its magnificent mountains, sequestered vales and verdant lined lakes and bays, and ever yearn in tender, fond affection over the lonely hearted living, and often return from the Happy Hunting Ground to visit, guide, console and comfort them.

Day and night cannot dwell together. The Red Man has ever fled the approach of the White Man, as the morning mists flees before the morning sun.

However, your proposition seems fair and I think that my people will accept it and will retire to the reservation you offer them. Then we will dwell apart in peace, for the words of the Great White Chief seem to be the words of nature speaking to my people out of the dense darkness.

It matters little where we pass the remnant of our days. They will not be many. The Indians' night promises to be dark. Not a single star of hope hovers above his horizon. Sad-voiced winds moan in the distance. Grim fate seems to be on the Red Man's Trail, and wherever he goes he will hear the approaching footsteps of his fell destroyer and prepare to stolidly meet his doom, as does the wounded doe that hears the approaching footsteps of the hunter.

A few more moons. A few more winters--and not one of the descendants of the mighty hosts that once moved over this broad land or lived in happy homes, protected by the Great Spirit, will remain to mourn over the graves of a people--once more powerful and hopeful than yours. But why should I mourn at the untimely fate of my people? Tribe follow tribe, and nation follows nation, like the waves of the sea. It is the order of nature, and regret is useless. Your time of decay may be distant, but it will surely come, for even the White Man whose God walked and talked with him as friend with friend, can not be exempt from the common destiny. We may be brothers after all. We shall see.

We will ponder your proposition and when we decide we will let you know. But should we accept it, I here and now make this condition that we will not be denied the privilege without molestation of visiting at any time the tombs of our ancestors, friends and children.

Every part of this soil is sacred in the estimation of my people. Every hillside, every valley, every plain and grove, has been hallowed by some sad or happy event in days long vanished. Even the rocks, which seem to be dumb and dead as they swelter in the sun along the silent shore, thrill with memories of stirring events connected with the lives of my people, and the very dust upon which you now stand responds more lovingly to their footsteps than to yours, because it is rich with the blood of our ancestors and our bare feet are conscious of the sympathetic touch. Our departed braves, and fond mothers, glad, happy-hearted maidens, and even the little children who lived here and rejoiced here for a brief season, will love these somber solitudes and at eventide they greet shadowy returning spirits. And when the last Red Man shall have perished, and the memory of my tribe shall have become a myth among the White Men, these shores shall swarm with the invisible dead of my tribe, and when your children's children shall think themselves alone in the field, the store, the shop, upon the highway, or in the silence of the pathless woods, they will not be alone. In all the earth there is no place dedicated to solitude. At night when the streets of your cities and villages are silent and you think them deserted, they will throng with the returning hosts that once filled them and still love this beautiful land. The White Man will never be alone.

Let him be just and deal kindly with my people, for the dead are not powerless. Dead, did I say? There is no death. Only a change of worlds.

APPENDIX 6

Version 2

Translated By William Arrowsmith[357]

1969

Brothers: That sky above us has pitied our fathers for many hundreds of years. To us it looks unchanging, but it may change. Today it is fair. Tomorrow it may be covered with cloud.

My words are like the stars. They do not set. What Seattle says, the great chief Washington can count on as surely as our white brothers can count on the return of the seasons.

The White Chief's son says his father sends us words of friendship and goodwill. This is kind of him, since we know he has little need of our friendship in return. His people are many, like the grass that covers the plains. My people are few, like the trees scattered by the storms on the grasslands.

The great--and good, I believe--White Chief sends us word that he wants to buy our land. But he will reserve us enough so that we can live comfortably. This seems generous, since the red man no longer has rights he need to respect. It may also be wise, since we no longer need a large country. Once my people covered this land like a flood-tide moving with the wind across the shell-littered flats. But that time is gone, and with it the greatness of tribes now almost forgotten.

But I will not mourn the passing of my people. Nor do I blame our white brothers for causing it. We too were perhaps partly to blame. When our young men grow angry at some wrong, real or imagined, they make their faces ugly with black paint. Then their hearts too are

---

[357]"Speech of Chief Seattle," *Arion* 8:461-464, 1969

ugly and black. They are hard and their cruelty knows no limits. And our old men cannot restrain them.

Let us hope that the wars between the red man and his white brothers will never come again. We would have everything to lose and nothing to gain. Young men view revenge as gain, even when they lose their own lives. But the old men who stay behind in time of war, mothers with sons to lose--they know better.

Our great father Washington--for he must be our father now as well as yours, since George has moved his boundary northward--our great and good father sends word by his son, who is surely a great chief among his people, that he will protect us if we do what he wants. His brave soldiers will be a strong wall for my people, and his great warships will fill our harbors. Then our ancient enemies to the north-- the Hadias and Tsimshians--will no longer frighten our women and old men. Then he will be our father and we will be his children.

But can that ever be? Your God loves your people and hates mine. He puts his strong arm around the white man and leads him by the hand, as a father leads his little boy. He has abandoned his red children. He makes your people stronger every day. Soon they will flood all the land. But my people are an ebb tide, we will never return. No, the white man's God cannot love his red children or he would protect them. Now we are orphans. There is no one to help us.

So how can we be brothers? How can your father be our father, and make us prosper and send us dreams of future greatness? Your God is prejudiced. He came to the white man. We never saw him, never even heard his voice. He gave the white man laws, but he had no word for his red children whose numbers once filled this land as the stars filled the sky.

No, we are two separate races, and we must stay separate. There is little in common between us.

To us the ashes of our fathers are sacred. Their graves are holy ground. But you are wanderers, you leave your fathers' graves behind you, and you do not care.

Your religion was written on tables of stone by the iron finger of an angry God, so you would not forget it. The red man could never understand it or remember it. Our religion is the ways of our forefathers, the dreams of our old men, sent them by the Great Spirit, and visions of our sachems. And it is written in the hearts of our people.

Your dead forget you and the country of their birth as soon as they go beyond the grave and walk among the stars. They are quickly forgotten and they never return. Our dead never forget this beautiful earth. It is their mother. They always love and remember her rivers, her great mountains, her valleys. They long for the living, who are lonely too and who long for the dead. And their spirits often return to visit and console us.

No, day and night cannot live together.

The red man has always retreated before the advancing white man, as the mist on the mountain slopes runs before the morning sun.

So your offer seems fair, and I think my people will accept it and go to the reservation you offer them. We will live apart, and in peace. For the words of the Great White Chief are like the words of nature speaking to my people out of the great darkness--a darkness that gathers around us like the night fog moving inland from the sea.

It matters little where we pass the rest of our days. They are not many. The Indians' night will be dark. No bright star shines on his horizons. The wind is sad. Fate hunts the red man down. Wherever he goes, he will hear the approaching steps of his destroyer, and prepare to die, like the wounded doe who hears the step of the hunter.

A few more moons, a few more winters, and none of the children of the great tribes that once lived in this wide earth or that roam now in small bands in the woods will be left to mourn the graves of a people once as powerful and as hopeful as yours.

But why should I mourn the passing of my people? Tribes are made of men, nothing more. Men come and go, like the waves of the sea. A tear, a prayer to the Great Spirit, a dirge, and they are gone from our longing eyes forever. Even the white man, whose God walked and talked with him as friend to friend, cannot be exempt from the common destiny.

We may be brothers after all. We shall see.

We will consider your offer. When we have decided, we will let you know. Should we accept, I here and now make this condition: we will never be denied the right to visit, at any time, the graves of our fathers and our friends.

Every part of this earth is sacred to my people. Every hillside, every valley, every clearing and wood, is holy in the memory and experience of my people. Even those unspeaking stones along the shore are loud with the events and memories in the life of my people. The ground beneath your feet responds more lovingly to our steps than yours, because it is the ashes of our grandfathers. Our bare feet know the kindred touch. The earth is rich with the lives of our kin.

The young men, the mothers, and girls, the little children who once lived and were happy here, still love these lonely places. And at evening the forests are dark with the presence of the dead. When the last red man has vanished from this earth, and his memory is only a story among the whites, these shores will still swarm with the invisible dead of my people. And when your children's children think they are alone in the fields, the forests, the shops, the highways, or the quiet of the woods, they will not be alone. There is no place in this country where a man can be alone. At night when the streets of your towns and cities are quiet, and you think they are empty, they will throng with the returning spirits that once thronged them, and still love those places. The white man will never be alone.

So let him be just and deal kindly with my people. The dead have power too.

APPENDIX 7

Version 3

Written by Ted Perry[358]

1970

Every part of this earth is sacred to my people. Every shining pine needle, every tender shore, every vapor in the dark woods, every clearing, and every humming insect are holy in the memory and experience of my people. The sap which courses through the trees carries the memories of the red man.

The white man's dead forget the country of their birth when they walk among the stars. Our dead never forget this beautiful earth, for it is the mother of the red men. Our dead always love and remember the earth's swift rivers, the silent footsteps of spring, the sparkling ripples on the surface of the ponds, the gaudy colors of the birds. We are a part of the earth and it is a part of us. The perfumed flowers are our sisters; the deer, the horse, the great condor, these are our brothers. The rocky crests, the juices in the meadows, the body heat of the pony, and man--all belong to the same family.

So when the Great Chief in Washington sends word that he wishes to buy our land, he asks much of us.

What Chief Seattle says, the Great Chief in Washington can count on as surely as our white brothers can count on the return of the seasons. My words are like the stars. They do not set.

Chief Washington also sends us words of friendship and goodwill. This is kind of him.

So we will consider your offer to buy our land. It will not be easy. This land is sacred to us. We take our pleasure in the woods and

---

[358]The original long text delivered to John Stevens, the producer of the film, HOME.

the dancing streams. The water that moves in the brooks is not water but the blood of our ancestors. If we sell you the land, you must remember that it is sacred to us, and forever teach your children that it is sacred. Each ghostly reflection in the clear water of the lakes tells of events and memories in the life of my people. The water's gurgle is the voice of my father's father. The rivers are our brothers; they quench our thirst. The rivers, between the tender arms of their banks, carry our canoes where they will. If we sell our land, you must remember, and teach your children, that the rivers are our brothers, and yours, and you must henceforth give the rivers the kindness you would give to any brother.

So Chief Seattle will consider the offer of Chief Washington. We will consider. The red man has always retreated before the advancing white man, as the mist on the mountain slopes runs before the morning sun. To us the ashes of our fathers are sacred. Their graves are holy ground, and so these hills, these trees. This portion of earth is consecrated to us. The white man does not understand. One portion of land is the same to him as the next, for he is a wanderer who comes in the night and borrows from the land whatever he needs. The earth is not his brother, but his enemy, and when he has won the struggle, he moves on. He leaves his father's graves behind, and he does not care. He kidnaps the earth from his children. And he does not care. The father's graves and the children's birthright are forgotten by the white man, who treats his mother the earth and his brother the sky as things to be bought, plundered, and sold, like sheep, bread, or bright beads. In this way, the dogs of appetite will devour the rich earth and leave only a desert.

The white man is like a snake who eats his own tail in order to live. And the tail grows shorter and shorter.

Our ways are different from your ways. We do not live well in your cities, which seem like so many black warts on the face of the earth. The sight of the white man's cities pains the eyes of the red man like the sunlight which stabs the eyes of one emerging from a dark cave. There is no place in the white man's cities quiet enough to hear the unfurling of leaves in Spring or the rustle of insects' wings. In the white man's cities, one is always trying to outrun an avalanche. The clatter only seems to pierce the ears. But what is there to living if a man cannot hear the lonely cry of the thrush or the arguments of the frogs around a pond at night? But I am a red man and do not understand. I prefer the wind darting over the face of a pond and the smell of the wind itself, cleansed by a midday rainshower. The air is precious to the red man, for all things share the same breath--the beasts, the trees, and man, they are all of the same breath. The white man does not mind the foul air he breathes. Like a man in pain for many days, he is numb to the stench. But if we sell our land, you must remember that the air is precious to us, and our trees, and the beasts. The wind gives man his first breath and receives his last sigh. And if we sell you our land, you will keep it apart and sacred, as a place where even the white man can go to taste a wind sweetened by meadow flowers.

So we will consider your offer to buy our land. If we decide to accept, I will here and now make one condition: the white man must treat the beasts of this land as his brothers.

I have heard stories of a thousand rotting buffaloes on the prairie, left by the white men who shot them from a passing train. I do not understand. For us, the beasts are our brothers, and we kill only to stay alive. If we sell him this land, the white man must do the same, for the animals are our brothers. What is man without the beast? Even the earthworm keeps the earth soft for man to walk upon. If all the beasts were gone, men would die from great loneliness. For whatever happens to the beasts, happens to man--for we are all of one breath. We will consider your offer to buy our land. Do not send men asking us to decide more quickly. We will decide in our time. Should we accept, I here and now make this condition: we will never be denied the right to walk softly over the graves of our fathers, mothers, and friends, nor may the white man desecrate these graves.

The graves must always be open to the sunlight and the falling rain. Then the water will fall gently upon the green sprouts and seep slowly down to moisten the parched tips of our ancestors and quench their thirst. If we sell this land to you, I will make now this condition: You must teach your children that the ground beneath their feet responds more lovingly to our steps than to yours, because it is rich with the lives of our kin. Teach your children what we have taught our children, that the earth is our mother. Whatever befalls the earth, befalls the sons of the earth. If men spit upon the ground, they spit upon themselves. This we know. The earth does not belong to the white man, the white man belongs to the earth. This we know. All things are connected like the blood which unites our family. If we kill the snakes, the field mice will multiply and destroy our corn. All things are connected. Whatever befalls the earth, befalls the sons and daughters of earth. Man did not weave the web of life; he is merely a strand in it. Whatever he does to the web, he does to himself.

No, day and night cannot live together. We will consider your offer. What is it that the white man wishes to buy, my people ask me? The idea is strange to us. How can you buy or sell the sky, the warmth of the land, the swiftness of the antelope? How can we sell these things to you and how can you buy them? Is the earth yours to do with as you will, merely because the red man signs a piece of paper and gives it to the white man? If we do not own the freshness of the air and the sparkle of the water, how can you buy them from us? Can you buy back the buffalo, once the last one has died? But we will consider your offer. In his passing moment of strength, the white man thinks that he is a god who can treat his mother (the earth), the rivers (which are his sisters), and his red brothers, as he wishes. But the man who would buy and sell his mother, his brothers, and sisters would also burn his children to keep himself warm.

So we will consider your offer to buy our land. Day and night cannot live together. Your offer seems fair, and I think my people will accept it and go to the reservation you have for them. We will live apart, and in peace.

Tribes are made of men, nothing more. Men come and go, like the waves of the sea. The whites too shall pass; perhaps sooner than all other tribes. Continuing to contaminate his own bed, the white man will one night suffocate in his own filth.

But in his perishing the white man will shine brightly, fired by the strength of the god who brought him to this land and for some special purpose gave him dominion over this land. That destiny is a mystery to us, for we do not understand what living becomes when the buffalo are all slaughtered, the wild horses all tamed, the secret corners of the forest are heavy with the scent of many men, and the view of the ripe hills blotted by talking wires. Where is the thicket? Gone. Where is the eagle? Gone. And what is it to say goodbye to the swift pony and the hunt? The end of living and the beginning of survival.

The white man's god gave him dominion over the beasts, the woods, and the red man, and for some special purpose, but that destiny is a mystery to the red man. We might understand if we knew what it was that the white man dreams, what hopes he describes to children on long winter nights, what visions he burns onto their eyes so that they will wish for tomorrow. The white man's dreams are hidden from us. And because they are hidden, we will go our own way.

So we will consider your offer to buy our land. If we agree, it will be to secure the reservation you have promised. There, perhaps, we may live out our brief days as we wish. There is little in common between us.

If we sell you our land, it will be filled with the bold young men, the warmbreasted mothers, the sharp-minded women, and the little children who once lived and were happy here.

Your dead go to walk among the stars, but our dead return to the earth they love. The white man will never be alone unless, in some distant day, he destroys the mountains, the trees, the rivers, and the air. If the earth should come to that, and the spirits of our dead, who love the earth, no longer wish to return and visit their beloved, then in that noon glare that pierces the eyes, the white man will walk his desert in great loneliness.

APPENDIX 8

Version 3 A

Edited by John Stevens[359]

1971

Southern Baptist Radio & Television's Version

of Ted Perry's Script

Narration adapted from a speech by Chief Seattle of the Duwamish Tribe, Washington Territory in 1855, when Indians were still the people of dreams and believed their land and their destiny to be inseparable. [360]

The Great Chief in Washington sends word that he wishes to buy our land.

The Great Chief also sends us words of friendship and goodwill. This is kind of him, since we know he has little need of our friendship in return. But we will consider your offer. For we know that if we do not sell, the white man may come with guns and take our land.

How can you buy or sell the sky, the warmth of the land? The idea is strange to us.

If we do not own the freshness of the air and the sparkle of the water, how can you buy them from us?

---

[359]Film script of <u>HOME</u> from Television Series THE HUMAN DIMENSION as edited by John Stevens, the producer of the film working for The Southern Baptist Convention Radio & Television Commission.
[360]The foreword was edited by John Stevens.

We will decide in our time.

What Chief Seattle says, the Great Chief in Washington can count on as truly as our white brothers can count on the return of the seasons. My words are like the stars. They do not set.

Every part of this earth is sacred to my people. Every shining pine needle, every sandy shore, every mist in the dark woods, every clearing, and humming insect is holy in the memory and experience of my people. The sap which courses through the trees carries the memories of the red man.

The white man's dead forget the country of their birth when they go to walk among the stars. Our dead never forget this beautiful earth, for it is the mother of the red man.

We are part of the earth and it is part of us. The perfumed flowers are our sisters the deer, the horse, the great eagle, these are our brothers, The rocky crests, the juices in the meadows, the body heat of the pony, and man--all belong to the same family.

So, when the Great Chief in Washington sends word that he wishes to buy our land, he asks much of us.

The Great Chief sends word he will reserve us a place so that we can live comfortably to ourselves. He will be our father and we will be his children.

But can that ever be? God loves your people, but has abandoned his red children. He sends machines to help the white man with his work, and builds great villages for him. He makes your people stronger every day. Soon you will flood the land like the rivers which crash down the canyons after a sudden rain. But my people are an ebbing tide, we will never return.

No, we are separate races. Our children do not play together and old men tell different stories. God favors you, and we are orphans.

So we will consider your offer to buy our land. But it will not be easy. For this land is sacred to us. We take our pleasure in these woods. I do not know. Our ways are different from your ways.

This shining water that moves in the streams and rivers is not just water but the blood of our ancestors. If we sell you land, you must remember that it is sacred, and that each ghostly reflection in the clear water of the lakes tells of events and memories in the life of my people. The water's murmur is the voice of my father's father.

The rivers are our brothers, they quench our thirst. The rivers carry our canoes, and feed our children. If we sell you our land, you must remember, and teach your children, that the rivers are our brothers, and yours, and you must henceforth give rivers the kindness you would give any brother.

The red man has always retreated before the advancing white man, as the mist of the mountain runs before the morning sun. But the ashes of our fathers are sacred. Their graves are holy ground, and so these hills, these trees, this portion of the earth is consecrated to us. We know that the white man does not understand our ways. One portion of land is the same to him as the next, for he is a stranger who comes in the night and takes from the land whatever he needs. The earth is not his brother but his enemy, and when he has conquered it, he moves on. He leaves his father's graves behind, and he does not care. He kidnaps the earth from his children. He does not care. His father's graves and his children's birthright are forgotten. He treats his mother, the earth, and his brother, the sky, as things to be bought, plundered, sold like sheep or bright beads. His appetite will devour the earth and leave behind only a desert.

I do not know. Our ways are different from your ways. The sight of your cities pains the eyes of the red man. But perhaps it is because the red man is savage and does not understand.

There is no quiet place in the white man's cities. No place to hear the unfurling of leaves in spring or the rustle of insect's wings. But perhaps it is because I am a savage and do not understand. The clatter only seems to insult the ears. And what is there to life if a man cannot hear the lonely cry of the whippoorwill [sic] or the arguments of the frogs around a pond at night? I am a red man and do not understand. The

Indian prefers the soft sound of the wind darting over the face of a pond, and the smell of the wind itself, cleansed by a midday rain, or scented with the pinon pine.

The air is precious to the red man, for all things share the same breath--the beast, the tree, the man, they all share the same breath. The white man does not seem to notice the air he breathes. Like a man dying for many days, he is numb to the stench. But if we sell our land, you must remember that the air is precious to us, that the air shares its spirit with all the life it supports. The wind that gave our grandfather his first breath also receives his last sigh. And the wind must also give our children the spirit of life. And if we sell you our land, you must keep it apart and sacred, as a place where even the white man can go to taste the wind that is sweetened by the meadow's flowers.

So we will consider your offer to buy our land. If we decide to accept, I will make one condition: The white man must treat the beasts of this land as his brothers.

I am a savage and I do not understand any other way. I have seen a thousand rotting buffalos on the prairie, left by the white man who shot them from a passing train. I am a savage and I do not understand how the smoking iron horse can be more important than the buffalo that we kill only to stay alive.

What is man without the beast? If all the beasts were gone, men would die from a great loneliness of spirit. For whatever happens to the beasts, soon happens to man. All things are connected.

Whatever befalls the earth befalls the sons of the earth.

You must teach your children that the ground beneath their feet is the ashes of our grandfathers. So that they will respect the land, tell your children that the earth is rich with the lives of our kin. Teach your children what we have taught our children, that the earth is our mother. Whatever befalls the earth, befalls the sons of the earth. If men spit upon the ground, they spit upon themselves.

This we know. The earth does not belong to man; man belongs to the earth. This we know. All things are connected like the blood, which unites one family. All things are connected.

Whatever befalls the earth befalls the sons of the earth. Man did not weave the web of life; he is merely a strand in it. Whatever he does to the web, he does to himself.

No, day and night cannot live together.

Our dead go to live in the earth's sweet rivers, they return with the silent footsteps of spring, and it is their spirit, running in the wind, that ripples the surface of the ponds.

We will consider why the white man wishes to buy the land. What is it that the white man wishes to buy, my people ask me. The idea is strange to us. How can you buy or sell the sky, the warmth of the land?--the swiftness of the antelope? How can we sell these things to you and how can you buy them? Is the earth yours to do with as you will, merely because the red man signs a piece of paper and gives it to the white man? If we do not own the freshness of the air and the sparkle of the water, how can you buy them from us.

Can you buy back the buffalo, once the last one has been killed? But we will consider your offer, for we know that if we do not sell, the white man may come with guns and take our land. But we are primitive, and in his passing moment of strength the white man thinks that he is a god who already owns the earth. How can a man own his mother?

But we will consider your offer to buy our land. Day and night cannot live together. We will consider your offer to go to the reservation you have for my people. We will live apart, and in peace. It matters little where we spend the rest of our days. Our children have seen their fathers humbled in defeat. Our warriors have felt shame, and after defeat they turn their days in idleness and contaminate their bodies with sweet foods and strong drink. It matters little where we pass the rest of our days. They are not many. A few more hours, a few more winters, and none of the children of the great tribes that once lived on this earth or that roam now in small bands in the woods will be left to mourn the graves of a people once as powerful and hopeful as yours.

But why should I mourn the passing of my people? Tribes are made of men, nothing more. Men come and go like the waves of the sea.

Even the white man, whose God walks and talks with him as friend to friend, cannot be exempt from the common destiny. We may be brothers after all; we shall see. One thing we know, which the white man may one day discover--our God is the same God.

You may think now that you own Him as you wish to own our land; but you cannot. He is the God of man, and His compassion is equal for the red man and the white. This earth is precious to Him, and to harm the earth is to heap contempt on its Creator. The whites too shall pass; perhaps sooner than all other tribes. Continue to contaminate your bed, and you will one night suffocate in your own waste.

But in your perishing you will shine brightly, fired by the strength of the God who brought you to this land and for some special purpose gave you dominion over this land and over the red man. That destiny is a mystery to us, for we do not understand when the buffalo are all slaughtered, the wild horses are tamed, the secret corners of the forest heavy with the scent of many men, and the view of the ripe hills blotted by talking wires. Where is the thicket? Gone. Where is the eagle? Gone. And what is it to say goodbye to the swift pony and the hunt? The end of living and the beginning of survival.

God gave you dominion over the beasts, the woods, and the red man, and for some special purpose, but that destiny is a mystery to the red man. We might understand if we knew what it was that the white man dreams--what hopes he describes to his children on long winter nights--what visions he burns onto their minds so that they will wish for tomorrow. But we are savages. The white man's dreams are hidden from us. And because they are hidden, we will go our own way. For above all else, we cherish the right of each man to live as he wishes, however different from his brothers. There is little in common between us.

So we will consider your offer to buy our land. If we agree, it will be to secure the reservation you have promised. There, perhaps, we may live out our brief days as we wish.

When the last red man has vanished from this earth, and his memory is only the shade of a cloud moving across the prairie, these shores and forests will still hold the spirits of my people. For they love this earth as the newborn loves its mother's heartbeat.

If we sell you our land, love it as we've loved it. Care for it as we've cared for it. Hold in your mind the memory of the land as it is when you take it. And with all your strength, with all your mind, with all your heart, preserve it for your children, and love it . . . . as God loves us all.

One thing we know. Our God is the same God. This earth is precious to Him. Even the white man cannot be exempt from the common destiny. We may be brothers after all. We shall see.

APPENDIX 9

Version 3

Friends of the Earth

and

"This earth is sacred"[361]

Environmental Action

November 11, 1972

The following letter, written in 1855, was sent to President Franklin Pierce by Chief Sealth of the Duwamish Tribe of the State of Washington. It concerns the proposed purchase of the tribe's land. Seattle, a corruption of the chief's name, is built in the heart of Duwamish land. The letter is printed courtesy of Dale Jones of the Seattle office of Friends of the Earth.
　　　　The Great Chief in Washington sends word that he wishes to buy our land. The Great Chief also sends us words of friendship and goodwill. This is kind of him, since we know he has little need of our friendship in return. But we will consider your offer, for we know that if we do not so, the white man may come with guns and take our land. What Chief Sealth says, the Great Chief in Washington can count on as truly as our white brothers can count on the return of the seasons. My words are like stars - they do not set.
　　　　How can you buy or sell the sky - the warmth of the land? The idea is strange to us. Yet we do not own the freshness of the air or the sparkle of the water. How can you buy them from us? We will decide in our time. Every part of this earth is sacred to my people. Every

---

[361]"This earth is sacred," *Environmental Action*, 11 November 1972, 7.

shining pine needle, every sandy shore, every mist in the dark woods, every clearing, and humming insect is holy in the memory and experience of my people.

We know that the white man does not understand our ways. One portion of land is the same to him as the next, for he is a stranger who comes in the night and takes from the land whatever he needs. The earth is not his brother, but his enemy, and when he has conquered it, he moves on. He leaves his father's graves, and his children's birthright is forgotten. The sight of your cities pains the eyes of the redman. But perhaps it is because the red man is savage and does not understand . . .

There is no quiet place in the white man's cities. No place to hear the unfurling of leaves of spring or the rustle of insect's wings. But perhaps because I am a savage and do not understand - the clatter only seems to insult the ears. And what is there to life if a man cannot hear the lovely cry of the whippoorwill or the arguments of the frogs around a pond at night? The Indian prefers the soft sound of the wind darting over the face of a pond, and the smell of the wind itself cleansed by a mid-day rain, or scented with the pinon pine. The air is precious to the redman. For all things share the same breath - the beasts, the trees, the man. The white man does not seem to notice the air he breathes. Like a man dying for many days, he is numb to the stench.

If I decide to accept, I will make one condition. The white man must treat the beasts of this land as his brothers. I am a savage and I do not understand any other way. I have seen a thousand rotting buffaloes on the prairie left by the white man who shot them from a passing train. I am a savage and I do not understand how the smoking iron horse can be more important than the buffalo that we kill only to stay alive. What is man without the beast? If all the beasts were gone, men would die from a great loneliness of spirit, for whatever happens to the beasts also happens to man. All things are connected. Whatever befalls the earth befalls the sons of the earth.

Our children have seen their fathers humbled in defeat. Our warriors have felt shame. And after defeat, they turn their days in idleness and contaminate their bodies with sweet food and strong drink. It matters little where we pass the rest of our days - they are not many. A few more hours, a few more winters, and none of the children of the great tribes that once lived on this earth or that roamed in small bands in the woods, will be left to mourn the graves of a people once as powerful and hopeful as yours.

One thing we know which the white man may one day discover. Our God is the same God. You may think now that you own him as you wish to own our land. But you cannot. He is the Body of man. And his compassion is equal for the redman and the white. This earth is precious to him. And to harm the earth is to heap contempt on its creator. The whites, too, shall pass - perhaps sooner than all other tribes. Continue to contaminate your bed, and you will one night suffocate in your own waste. When the buffalo are all slaughtered, the wild horses are tamed, the secret corners of the forest heavy with the scent of many men, and the view of the ripe hills blotted by talking wires, where is the thicket? Gone. Where is the eagle? Gone. And what is it to say goodby [sic] to the swift and the hunt, the end of living and the beginning of survival.

We might understand if we knew what it was that the white man dreams, what hopes he describes to his children on long winter nights, what visions he burns into their minds, so they will wish for tomorrow. But we are savages. The white man's dreams are hidden from us. And because they are hidden, we will go our own way. If we agree, it will be to secure your reservation you have promised. There, perhaps we may live out our brief days as we wish. When the last redman has vanished from this earth, and the memory is only the shadow of a cloud moving across the prairie, these shores and forests will still hold the spirits of my people, for they love this earth as the newborn loves its mother's heartbeat. If we sell you our land, love it as we've loved it. Care for it, as we've cared for it. Hold in your mind the memory of the land, as it is when you take it. And with all your strength, with all your might, with all your heart - preserve it for your children, and love it as God loves us all. One thing we know - our God is the same. This earth is precious to him. Even the white man cannot be exempt from the common destiny.

155

APPENDIX 10

Version 3

Wildlife Omnibus

November 15, 1973[362]

IN 1855, Chief Sealth of the Duwamish Tribe of the state of Washington sent a letter to President Franklin Pierce concerning the proposed purchase of the tribe's land. "Continue to contaminate your bed," the Indian chief warned, "and one night you will suffocate in your own waste. When the buffalo are all slaughtered, the wild horses all tamed, the secret corners of the forest heavy with the scent of many men, and the view of the ripe hills blotted by talking wires, where is the thicket? Gone. Where is the eagle? Gone . . . If we sell you our land, love it as we loved it. . . . Hold in your mind the memory of the land as it is when you take it. And with all your strength, all your might, an with all your heart, preserve it for your children."

Shortly after these words were written, the sale of the lands was made final. Ironically, the city of Seattle--one of the nation's cleanest urban areas--now stands in the heart of Duwamish country.

---

[362]"For your children," *Wildlife Omnibus*, 15 November 1973, 30.

APPENDIX 11

Version 4

Anonymous Author[363]

Spokane Expo

1974

The President in Washington sends word that he wishes to buy our land.

Buy our land!
But how can you buy or sell the sky, the land?
The idea is strange to us. If we do not own the freshness of the air and the sparkle of the water, how can you buy them?

Every part of this earth is sacred to my people.
Every shining pine needle,
every sandy shore, every mist in the dark woods, every meadow,
every humming insect.
All is Holy in the memory and experience of my people.

We know the sap which courses through the trees as we know the blood that courses through our veins.
We are part of the earth and it is part of us.

The perfumed flowers are our sisters.
The bear, the deer, the great eagle,

---

[363]Written for The Spokane Expo of 1974.

these are our brothers.

The rocky crests, the juices in the meadows,
the body heat of the pony,--and man,
all belong to the same family.

The shining water that moves in the streams and rivers is not just water, but the blood of our ancestors.

If we sell you land you must remember that it is sacred.
Each ghostly reflection in the clear water of the lakes
tell of events and memories in the life of my people.
The water's murmur is the voice of my father's father.

The rivers--they are our brothers.
They quench our thirst.
They carry our canoes, they feed our children.
So, you must give to rivers the kindness you would give any brother.

If we sell you our land, remember that the air is precious to us,
that the air shares its spirit with all life it supports.
It is the wind that gave our grandfather his first breath.
It is the wind that receives his last sigh.

The wind also gives our children the spirit of life.
So, if we sell you our land, you must keep it apart as a place
where man can go and experience the Sacred.

Keep the land as a place where man can go to taste the wind
that is sweetened by the meadow flowers.

Will you teach your children what we have taught our children?
That the earth is our mother?

Whatever befalls the earth, befalls all the sons of the earth.

This we know:
The earth does not belong to man, man belongs to the earth.
All things are connected like the blood which unites us all.

Man did not weave the web of life, he is merely a strand in it.
Whatever he does to the web, he does to himself.

One thing we know:
Our God is also your God.
We both know the earth is precious to Him and to harm the earth
is to heap contempt on its Creator

Your destiny is a mystery to us.
What will happen when the buffalo are all slaughtered? The wild horses
tamed?
What will happen when the secret corners of the forest are heavy with
the scent of many men?
What we will happen when the view of the ripe hills is blotted by
talking wires?
Where will the thicket be? Gone.
Where will the eagle be? Gone.
And what is it to say goodbye to the swift pony and the hunt?
That would be the end of living and the beginning of surviving.

When the last red man has vanished with the wilderness
and his memory is only the shadow of a cloud moving across the
prairie, will these shores and forests still be here?
Will there be any of the spirit of my people left?

We love this earth as a newborn loves its mother's heartbeat.
So, if we sell you our land, love it as we have loved it.
Care for it as we cared for it.
Hold it in your mind.
Keep forever the memory of the land as it is when you receive it.
Preserve the land for all children and love it.

As we are part of the land, you too are part of the land.
This earth is precious to us. It is also precious to you.

No man, be he red man or white man can be apart.

One thing we know:
There is only one God. We are all brothers.

APPENDIX 12

Version 4 A

Anonymous Author

"The Decidedly Unforked Message Of Chief Seattle"[364]

1974

Chief Seattle, leader of the Suquamish tribe in the Washington territory, delivered a speech prophetic, in 1854, to mark the transferral of ancestral Indian lands to the federal government. An adaptation of his remarks, based on an English translation by William Arrowsmith, appears at right.

More than 100 years later, his words have an eerie ring of truth and are punctuated by the energy crisis which shadows the land. Having recently learned that our technology can kill our environment, including us, will we throw much of that lesson to the winds in a mad scramble for energy at any price?

Expo '74 was created with the idea that we, in our highly mechanized society, can indeed live in harmony with our land and all life. Chief Seattle saw no distinction between life and the earth. One of the major failings of people in this age is drawing a deadly imaginary line between the two. Perhaps the thought generated by Expo '74 will help erase it.

Visitors entering the U.S. Pavilion will be confronted by a quotation from Chief Seattle's speech--"The earth does not belong to man; man belongs to the earth." Those are not idle words. Let's not be idle about observing their wisdom . . . to the letter.

The Great Chief in Washington sends word that he wishes to buy our land.

---

[364]"The Decidedly Unforked Message Of Chief Seattle," *Northwest Airline Magazine - Passages*, April, 1974.

The Great Chief also sends us words of friendship and good will. This is kind of him, since we know he has little need of our friendship in return. But we will consider your offer. For we know that if we do not sell, the white man may come with guns and take our land.

How can you buy or sell the sky, the warmth of the land? The idea is strange to us.

If we do not own the freshness of the air and the sparkle of the water, how can you buy them?

Every part of this earth is sacred to my people. Every shining pine needle, every sandy shore, every mist in the dark woods, every clearing, and humming insect is holy in the memory and experience of my people. The sap which courses through the trees carries the memories of the red man.

The white man's dead forget the country of their birth when they go to walk among the stars. Our dead never forget this beautiful earth, for it is the mother of the red man. We are part of the earth and it is part of us. The perfumed flowers are our sisters; the deer, the horse, the great eagle, these are our brothers. The rocky crests, the juices in the meadows, the body heat of the pony, and man--all belong to the same family.

So, when the Great Chief in Washington sends word that he wishes to buy our land, he asks much of us.

The Great Chief sends word he will reserve us a place so that we can live comfortably to ourselves. He will be our father and we will be his children.

So we will consider your offer to buy our land. But it will not be easy. For this land is sacred to us.

This shining water that moves in the streams and rivers is not just water but the blood of our ancestors. If we sell you land, you must remember that it is sacred, and you must teach your children that it is sacred, and that each ghostly reflection in the clear water of the lakes tells of events and memories in the life of my people. The water's murmur is the voice of my father's father.

The rivers are our brothers, they quench our thirst. The rivers carry our canoes, and feed our children. If we sell you our land, you must remember, and teach your children, that the rivers are our brothers, and yours, and you must henceforth give the rivers the kindness you would give any brother.

The red man has always retreated before the advancing white man, as the mist of the mountain runs before the morning sun. But the ashes of our fathers are scared. Their graves are holy ground and so these hills, these trees, this portion of the earth is consecrated to us. We know that the white man does not understand our ways. One portion of land is the same to him as the next, for he is a stranger who comes in the night and takes from the land whatever he needs. The earth is not his brother, but his enemy, and when he has conquered it, he moves on. He leaves his father's graves behind, and he does not care. He kidnaps the earth from his children. He does not care. His father's graves and his children's birthright are forgotten. He treats his mother, the earth, and his brother, the sky, as things to be bought, plundered, sold like sheep or bright beads. His appetite will devour the earth and leave behind only a desert.

I do not know. Our ways are different from your ways. The sight of your cities pains the eyes of the red man. But perhaps it is because the red man is a savage and does not understand.

There is no quiet place in the white man's cities. No place to hear the unfurling of leaves in spring or the rustle of insect's wings. But perhaps it is because I am a savage and do not understand. The clatter only seems to insult the ears. And what is there to life if a man cannot hear the lonely cry of the whippoorwill or the arguments of the frogs around a pond at night? I am a red man and do not understand. The Indian prefers the soft sound of the wind darting over the face of a pond, and the smell of the wind itself, cleansed by a midday rain or scented with the pinon pine.

The air is precious to the red man, for all things share the same breath -- the beast, the tree, the man, they all share the same breath. The white man does not seem to notice the air he breathes. Like a man dying for many days, he is numb to the stench. But if we sell you our land, you must remember that the air is precious to us, that the air shares its spirit with all the life it supports. The wind that gave our grandfather his first breath also receives his last sigh. And the wind must also give our children the spirit of life. And if we sell you our land, you must keep it apart and sacred, as a place where even the white man can go to taste the wind that is sweetened by the meadow's flowers.

So we will consider your offer to buy our land. If we decide to accept, I will make one condition: The white man must treat the beasts of this land as his brothers.

I am a savage and I do not understand any other way. I have seen a thousand rotting buffalos on the prairie, left by the white man who shot them from a passing train. I am a savage and I do not understand how the smoking iron horse can be more important than the buffalo that we kill only to stay alive.

What is man without the beasts? If all the beasts were gone, men would die from a great loneliness of spirit. For whatever happens to the beasts, soon happens to man. All things are connected.

You must teach your children that the ground beneath their feet is the ashes of our grandfathers. So that they will respect the land, tell your children that the earth is rich with the lives of our kin. Teach your children what we have taught our children, that the earth is our mother. Whatever befalls the earth, befalls the sons of the earth. If men spit upon the ground, they spit upon themselves.

This we know. The earth does not belong to man; man belongs to the earth. This we know. All things are connected like the blood which unites one family. All things are connected.

Whatever befalls the earth befalls the sons of the earth. Man did not weave the web of life; he is merely a strand in it. Whatever he does to the web, he does to himself.

But we will consider your offer to go to the reservation you have for my people. We will live apart and in peace. It matters little where we spend the rest of our days. Our children have seen their fathers humbled in defeat. Our warriors have felt shame, and after defeat they turn their days in idleness and contaminate their bodies with sweet foods and strong drink. It matters little where we pass the rest of our days. They are not many. A few more hours, a few more winters, and none of the children of the great tribes that once lived on this earth or that roam now in small bands in the woods will be left to mourn the graves of a people once as powerful and hopeful as yours. But why should I mourn, the passing of my people. Tribes are made of men, nothing more. Men come and go, like the waves of the sea.

Even the white man, whose God walks and talks with him as friend to friend, cannot be exempt from the common destiny. We may be brothers after all; we shall see. One thing we know, which the white man may one day discover--our God is the same God. You may think now that you own Him as you wish to own our land; but you cannot. He is the God of man, and His compassion is equal for the red man and the white. This earth is precious to Him, and to harm the earth is to heap contempt on its Creator. The whites too shall pass perhaps sooner than all other tribes. Continue to contaminate your bed, and you will one night suffocate in your own waste.

But in your perishing you will shine brightly fired by the strength of the God who brought you to this land and for some special purpose gave you dominion over this land and over the red man. That destiny is a mystery to us, for we do not understand when the buffalo are all slaughtered, the wild horses are tamed, the secret corners of the forest heavy with the scent of many men, and the view of the ripe hills blotted by talking wires. Where is the thicket? Gone. Where is the eagle? Gone. And what is it to say goodbye to the swift pony and the hunt? The end of living and the beginning of survival.

So we will consider your offer to buy our land. If we agree, it will be to secure the reservation your have promised. There, perhaps, we may live out our brief days as we wish. When the last red man has vanished from this earth, and his memory is only the shadow of a cloud moving across the prairie, these shores and forests will still hold the spirits of my people. For they love this earth as the newborn loves its mother's heartbeat. So if we sell you our land, love it as we've loved it. Care for it as we've cared for it. Hold in your mind the memory of the land as it is when you take it. And with all your strength, with all your mind, with all your heart, preserve it for your children, and love it . . . as God loves us all.

One thing we know. Our God is the same God. This earth is precious to Him. Even the white man cannot be exempt from the common destiny. We may be brothers after all. We shall see.

APPENDIX 13

Seathl's Name

Chief Seathl, Sealth or Sealt is commonly and incorrectly spelled Seattle. "It may have been after this triumph [he led an ambush that defeated a large war party about to attack his village] he assumed the name see-YAHTLH, the name of his father's father at a grand potlatch." [365] The tribal chairman for the Suquamish, Lawrence Webster, said, ". . . I can tell you one thing he wasn't named for either of his parents."[366] There is also evidence that it may have been spelled Tslalcom.

A Belgian priest Father A. Felix Verwilgen, living in the Seattle, was tracing the founding of St. George Industrial School for Indians when he uncovered references to a Chief Tslalakom. There were striking similarities between Chief Tslalakom and Chief Seathl. He found references to Tslalakom

> . . . in the early letters of the missionaries of the Diocese of Quebec, Frances Norbet Blanchet and Modeste Demers . . . In Report No. 2 of [Father] Blanchet we read (on the date of Sunday, May 31, 1840) ". . . Tslalakom also presented himself with the Sokwamish' [Suquamish]" . . . (Rapports sur les Missions etc., Jan, 1841; in the Eng. transl. p. 64). . . . From different references it is clear that Tslalakom is called especially the Chief of the Sokwamish [Suquamish].[367]

---

[365]David Buerge, "The Man We Call Seattle," *The Weekly*, 29 June - 5 July 1983, 24.

[366]Delores Tarzan, "A Tribal Tribute," *The Seattle Times*, 14 September 1983, B1.

[367]"Chief Sealth In the Letters of the First Christian Missionaries of the Puget Sound" (a paper presented by James Vernon Metcalfe for the Pioneer Association of

It appears from this quote that both men are considered chief's of the same tribe.

Father Verwilgen's second argument:

> is the authority of Tslalakom who is usually mentioned first, and takes the leading role at the reception of the missionaries . . . From the letters it seems evident that Tslalakom is the leading Chief in the Puget Sound, Area . . . There are said to be twelve chiefs of whom Tslalakom is only one, although he is the most prominent.[368]

A third argument is based on the location of the central village of Tslalakom. St. Peter's church, which is at present day Suquamish, has a cemetery with two gravestones dating back to 1842 and 1844. In a letter one of the Fathers writes of meeting Tslalakom at this site.[369] The last argument is that Chief Sealth and Chief Tslalakom both had the baptismal name of Noah.[370]

However, there is disagreement over this. Bill Holm, Curator of Northwest Coast Indian Art for the Thomas Burke Memorial Washington State Museum at the University of Washington, thinks, "On the subject of name 'Tslalacom,' I believe there is ample evidence for two men. There are many references to both Seattle and Tslalacom in the journals associated with the Hudson's Bay post at Fort Nisqually."[371]

Seathl's name has also "been recorded as Sealth, See Yat, See Yalt, Saw At, Se Alh, Stalhlil, See Alt, Talakum, or Tslalcom." The problem stems from the difficulty of Europeans to pronounce 'thl' which combines the English "th" and "l" sounds simultaneously by pushing the sound past either side of the tongue with enough force to

---

the State of Washington, May 1964), 1-4. Hereafter cited in the text as Verwilgen, "Christian Missionaries."

[368]Verwilgen, "Christian Missionaries."

[369]"(Rapports, p 60) in Vol. IV" quoted in Verwilgen, "Christian Missionaries," 2.

[370]The Catholic Northwest Progress, 18 December 1964, No.51, 7-10.

[371]Bill Holm, Seattle, to Janice Krenmayr, Seattle, 10 January 1975, Transcript at Seattle Museum of History and Industry, Seattle, Washington.

puff out your cheeks.[372] Frank Allen, a Skokomish Indian, pronounced Seathl's name s'iy'a`l. The interviewer William Elemendorf considered him in 1940 as "definitely a cultural conservative, almost a holdover from the pre-reservation generation of the days before the often-forced removal of Twana communities to the new Skokomish Reservations in the 1860's."[373] The vowels in s'iy'a`l are pronounced as follows: a as in father; i like vowel in pit; the modified vowel a` indicates a stressed vowel. The consonants are pronounced as follows: l like let; s like sand; and y like yes. The modified consonant "l is a voiceless lateral affricate, something like a tl in hotly, but unvoiced throughout. . ."[374]

---

[372]Janice Krenmayr, "'The earth is our mother' Who really said that'?," *The Seattle Times Sunday Magazine,* 5 January 1975, 4.

[373]Elmendorf, *Twana Narratives,* xxxv.

[374]Ibid., iv.

APPENDIX 14

Oral Traditions' Role

in

Historical Documentation

Seathl's war exploits and rise to "great chief" are based on oral history. Jan Vansina has written two books on the use of oral traditions for historical documentation. Although oral histories are rarely accurate word for word accounts of the past they are "representations of the past in the present. One cannot deny either the past or the present in them . . . Traditions must always be understood as reflecting both the past and the present in a single breath."[375] Oral traditions are messages at least a generation old. The stories of Seathl's early life are based on interviews of men who were his contemporaries. So the stories are not considered oral traditions. Vansina characterizes them as "news." "The main point is that such communication do *not* concern the past, but rather the present, and imply a future."[376] One of the many faults of eyewitness accounts is they "tend to report what they expect to see or hear more than what they actually see or hear. . . . Memory typically selects certain features from successive perceptions and interprets them according to expectation, previous knowledge, or the logic of 'what must have happened', and fills in the gaps."[377] Sam Coombs' interviews of warriors who witnessed Seathl's exploits are the basis for most of the accounts of his early adventures. Rather than discounting the warriors' accounts because of the inherent unreliability of eyewitness

---

[375] Jan Vansina, *Oral Tradition As History* (Madison, Wisconsin: University of Wisconsin Press, 1985), xii. See also: Vansina's, *A Study in Historical Methodology*, trans. H. M. Wright (Chicago: Aldine Publishing Co., 1961).
[376] Ibid., 4.
[377] Ibid., 5.

accounts, it forces the historian to look at them using a different criterion: "Ancient things are today . . . they are representations of the past in the present."[378] These oral histories of Seathl are evidence of Seathl's stature at the time the accounts were spoken. Whether or not they accurately reflect a detailed account of his exploits does not matter. What they do reflect is the esteem Seathl's people held for him and his leadership.

---

[378]Ibid., xii.

APPENDIX 15

Letter Sent by

Arrowsmith to Miller

In your letter you declare that a man with Smith's credentials would have been most unlikely to have "deliberately made up a hoax in a public article." But it is <u>not</u> my contention that Smith had perpetrated a hoax, whether you define "hoax" as a practical joke or a serious fraud. As I remarked to you on the phone there is a sizable body of late 19th Indian speeches purportedly produced by Indians but in fact ghost-written by white men.(The most famous of these perhaps is that of Chief Joseph's as it appeared in the <u>North American Review</u>; it gives us Joseph's sentiments but it has obviously been written by an editor of the journal. And there are many more of the same sort.).

The purpose of these ghosted speeches was not, for the most part, to deceive; or, if to deceive, to do so in the service of a benevolent end. I don't suppose I need to remind you that such verbal acts of sympathy, done for the putative benefit of waning tribal cultures, constantly recur. The commonest form of such acts was set speeches, usually attributed to an Indian of considerable fame: black Hawk, Tecumseh, Sitting Bull, Red Cloud, even Captain Jack. There were also acts of quite indefensible benevolent arrogance. The signature of Charlot, chief of the Flatlands, for instance, was forged on the paper that authorized the removal of his tribe from its ancestral home in the Bitterroot Range to the valley of the Jocko. The forgers included territorial governors and two American senators (one of them a future president of the United States); so much for respectability! The fraud was later uncovered by a Congressional investigating committee. While the forgers were obviously engaged in advancing their own political careers, they could also argue (and in fact did so) that, had Charlot's Flatlands been left to the mercy of the citizens of Missoula, the tribe would have been exterminated in a few short years; in the remoteness of the Jocko they were relatively safe. No need perhaps to labor the point; I simply want to indicate that there are forms of deceit (e.g., ghost-written Indian speeches) that are, in intention at least, altruistic and not in the least self-serving. Well-meaning whites wanted, if possible, to give Indian a "voice"---words that might, by their eloquence and understanding of the Indians' plight, impress and influence whites to change their attitudes and policies. Smith's speech belongs, I believe, to this category---a category which is in fact a fairly well-developed literary genre in the late 19th century. Smith's credentials for the genre were ideal: highly respected and well-placed, a professional man, educated, of unimpeachable integrity and social standing. He would have secured an immediate hearing for Seattle's people.

If you believe that the speech as reported by Smith is substantially what Seattle actually said, then how do you explain the allusions, the echoes and quotations from the classics of Western literature everywhere embedded in the text? You see, I am not at all impressed by your arguments from pioneer families and local historians, all of them writing considerably after the 1887 publication of Smith's Seattle. By that time I expect Smith's would have acquired its own aura of factuality, especially if Seattle did in fact give a speech in front of Maynard's. My evidence is the text of speech as reported by Smith. How, for instance, do you account for the echoes in it from, along others: Byron, Emerson. Milton, Jonathan Edwards, etc.? The only one of the white man's texts likely to be known to Seattle was the Bible. How then did these other texts get into Smith's speech? Whether they were consciously echoed by Smith or were simply allusions circulating unnoticed in his memory is irrelevant. And it seems to me quite inconceivable that Seattle somehow managed to come up with phrases which tally exactly with the words of Byron et al. Take, for instance, that vivid phrase in the Smith speech: "the iron finger of an angry God," What I hear in both the substance of the paragraph and the actual words of is the echo of Jonathan Edwards' notorious sermon, "Sinners in the Hands of an Angry God," exactly the sort of rigid puritanical text that would occur to a liberal Christian of "improving sentiment" like Smith---and also, I assume, to the educated readers of the Seattle Sunday Star. Well, I can hear you beginning to mutter, no doubt Smith did a little embellishing of his own, but the substance is still Seattle's. But there are so many embellishments, and their purpose (if indeed they are, as I suspect, quite <u>conscious</u> allusions----a tip to the educated among readers) is so transparent---to win the assent of whites by making Seattle's case in terms of words and themes borrowed from their own cultural texts---that embellishment simply won't wash. (Professor Kaiser, like a good German, doesn't recognize the problem because his own texts are German, not English; for Smith, Goethe and Schiller were presumably marginal authors). Anyway, if you add these echoes and allusions to Smith's Victorian locutions and "eloquence," and then link both to the quite unconscionable gap of almost forty-five years between the putative delivery of the speech by Seattle and Smith's publication of it, it is obvious that we have a very real problem of authenticity. Of the gap between delivery and publication, you provide, it seems to me, not even a minimally satisfactory explanation. It is my view that Smith made a few handwritten notes at the time of the speech and then put them aside. Later, when it became bleakly clear that Seattle's people were being threatened with extinction, Smith "worked up" the speech, expanding it by at least as much as Perry expanded my "translation" of Smith, and embellishing it thickly with texts that inhabited the white man's cultural memory. What better way to arouse a sense of conscience in the white man than to have an Indian speak to him in his own classic texts and the values implicit in those texts, all the great texts of human transience: Lo, how the mighty are fallen; pull down thy pride; Vanity, vanity, saith the preacher; For the days of man are like the leaves (or the grass or flowers); Be gentle, for your time may come (and we may be brothers after all). . .?

Smith's speech was obviously successful, at least as "literature." It created its own myth, even its own "facticity." That it cannot have been ghosted because, as you say, "everything of that nature would have been known in a small community" seems to me (I lived for many years in a small town in Vermont: <u>crede experto</u>) not only dubious but mistaken. No doubt members of small communities know more of their neighbors than do big-city dwellers; but for that very reason their secrets are nor jealously and ingeniously guarded. Haven't we all heard time again of some small-town hugger-mugger of which nobody but the village idiot knew, or of some crime unsuspected until suddenly, by accident, revealed? We have no disagreement about Smith's integrity. I doubt that it ever occurred to him that by giving Seattle a voice he had somehow committed a deception, Are historical novelists who invent conversations which never took place deceivers? Are deliberate fictions, masks, discrete disguises invariably the mark of the con-man or the fraud? Dubito. Smith could presumably have believed that his end justified his means (what else could have justified them?), just as the post-Perryean speechifiers in Texas seem to have been convinced that God's (Baptist) glory was privileged, and that the truth and historical fact were petty concerns when laid against the missionary imperative. But Smith's motives, at least by the moral standard and practice of the times, seem to me comparatively pure. He might well have deemed it his Christian duty to speak for Seattle and his people, even when enlarging generously on the chief's words. Certainly he could have comforted himself with the knowledge that better men than himself had not hesitated to labor in the ghost-writing vineyards.

Again, I simply don't recognize myself and my work in your charge that by adopting "a more contemporary [linguistic] usage", "I have lost "some of the spirituality of Sealth." And I deny that have unknowingly or unthinkingly "interjected several Euro-American concepts which Sealth [or Smith] did not mention." "Arrowsmith, you say, introduced the concept of Mother Earth which was not common in Indian cosmology [!!], especially in the Puget Sound tribes. Arrowsmith added this to the original [original???] text: 'Our dead never forget this beautiful earth. It is their mother. They always love and remember. . ."

I did not add: I unpacked what I thought was implied in Smith's phrase, "the world that gave them being." If the world gave them being, then surely the earth bore them, mothered them. In what way do you suppose the earth "gave them being"? Manufactured them? Sprouted them? What? And how have I thereby forfeited "spirituality"? Is Smith's phrase radiant with "the spirituality of Sealth"? What I am objecting to is your persistent suggestion that I am one of those popularizing white exploiters denounced by Means, writers who gabble sentimentally about "the Great Spirit" and the "Earthmother" And "Happy Hunting Grounds." And what, tell me, is your scholarly authority for the ludicrous statement that "the concept of Mother Earth was not common in Indian cosmology"? (Whether Earthmother sentiment was weak or strong among Puget Sound Indians, I simply can't say; you may be right, but by now I'm skeptical of your unsupported dogmatic statements). Your proffered evidence for this remarkable <u>canard</u> is a mysteriously uncited "collection of more than 200 speeches" in which, from 1609 to 1970, "the concept of Mother Earth was mentioned only one time." If, as I suspect, the author of this collection is Sam Gill, I am utterly unimpressed. Gill collects---i.e. selects---his speeches in such a way that they <u>must</u> produce the results he claims; that was why he selected <u>those</u> speeches. If the literally thousands of references to various Indian Earthmothers that crop up centrally in treaty negotiations and the speeches and statements attributed to Joseph, Peopeomoxmox, Black Hawk, Young Chief, Kamiakin, Smohalla, Homli, Stachas, etc. are to be treated as Gill treats them (mistranslations, misunderstanding, blind ethnocentrism); if every skilled translator (like those remarkable Canadian half-breeds who brought such linguistic skill to their work, every reporter, every professional observer---if they are <u>all</u> to be written off as unreliable, what evidence remains? All we have is the self-serving word of Sam Gill who, like so many of the literary theorists and revisionists these days, apparently thinks that his argument apply to everyone else, but not to himself. Whether I was right to suggest the presence of an Earthmother (no goddess in my thinking, simply the primal, fecund force of nature, the Great Matrix) in Seattle's words (or Smith's version of Seattle's words) I don't know; but I am dead certain that can't be censured on the basis of your remark (and/or Sam Gill's absurd thesis, quite properly trashed by the reviewer in <u>The Bloomsbury Review</u> you sent me). To take only a single example, that of Spokane (before the falls vanished into the generation of electricity). His answer, English, was: "This sky is my father. This earth is my mother. I will stay here until the white men push me out and out and out, until there is no more out." Gill's way of disposing of this would of course be to observe that Garry was "tailoring" his answer to the expectations of the delegation, that he really didn't believe the earth was his mother, etc. Against <u>that</u> way of arguing it is really impossible to appeal. For Gill, the thesis is true by definition; a real synthetic a priori proposition, a tautology. And I think I should tell you that you undermine your own authority by appealing to Gill or relying on his "findings."

What I resent is being discredited or written off as translating Smith's Seattle in terms of popular clichés. I <u>thought</u> about Earthmother, and not in the form of a "goddess." (By the way Means doesn't say that the concept doesn't exist, as you manage to suggest, but that he can't offer a unitary definition because it is so variously defined by different tribes). And I was in no way influenced by any Euro-American preconception, but rather by what I know and have read of Indian culture in the Northwest in the last four decades of the 19th century. I am not, I am trying to say, Russell Means' straw -man, the writer/commentator who isn't Indian and who therefore is guilty of all sorts of elementary blunders. And I dislike having to say so in my own defense. For your own (it seem to me) self-serving purposes, you tax me for introducing terms, which you assume I mean in the crassest and vacuous sense. And the effect, of course, is to laud yourself for being free of the faults you gratuitously ascribe to me. As for "Great Spirit," I stick to my guns. Anyone who has taken an entry-level anthropology course knows that the Amerindian concept in question is not to be rendered as "God." It is diffuse, universal <u>manna</u>, what the Greeks called, carefully differentiating it from the divine, the daimonic.

APPENDIX 16

Hazard Stevens' Sources for his book

Life of Isaac Stevens

The following is an exact copy of Stevens' page of sources.

Savage's New England Genealogies.

Abiel Abbott's History of Andover.

Miss Sarah Loring Bailey's Historical Sketches of Andover.

Church and town records of Andover.

Massachusetts Colonial Records.

Family records and correspondence.

History of the Mexican War, by General C. M. Wilcox.

Campaigns of the Rio Grande and of Mexico, by Major Isaac I. Stevens.

General Stevens's diary and letters (unpublished).

His reports in the Engineer Bureau of the Army (unpublished).

Reports of the Coast survey, Professor A.D. Bache, for 1850 to 1853.

Boston Post newspaper, files for 1852.

Pacific Railroad Routes Explorations, vols. i. and xii., two parts.

General Stevens's reports to Commissioner of Indian Affairs, with
journals of Indian councils and proceedings in 1854-55
(unpublished).

Reports of December 22, 1855, and January 29, 1856, in House
Document 48, 1st session, 34th Congress.

Reports of August 28, December 5, 1856, council at Fox
Island; October 22, 1856, second council at Walla Walla;
April 30, 1857, with map and census of Indian Tribes
(unpublished).

Reports to Jefferson Davis, Secretary of War, August 15, December
21, 1854; February 19, March 9 and 21, May 23 (two letters),
June 8, July 7 and 24, August 14, October 22, November 21
(three letters), 1856. See documents of 34th and 35th
Congresses.

Reports and correspondences of General Wool, Colonel George
Wright, and Lieutenant-Colonel Silas Casey, in said
documents.

Governor Stevens's messages to legislature of Washington Territory,
February 28, December 5, 1854; January 20, December, 1856,
the latter accompanied by reports to the Secretary of War and
correspondence with military officers during the Indian War.
See, also, above documents and messages for proceedings
relative to martial law.

Governor Stevens's speeches in 35th and 36th Congresses, in
Congressional Globe.

General Joseph Lane's speech in 35th Congress, May 13, 1858, on the
Indian War.

Three Years' Residence in Washington Territory, by James G. Swan.

The Walla Walla Council, by Colonel Lawrence Kip.

Account of Colonel Wright's campaign against the Spokanes, by Colonel Lawrence Kip.

Report of J. Ross Browne, Special Agent, etc., on the Indian war, House Document 58, 1st session, 35th Congress.

History of the Pacific States, by H. H. Bancroft, vols. xxiv.-xxvi.

Archives State Department.

Records War Department.

Circular Letter to Emigrants, the Northwest, Letter to the Vancouver Railroad Convention, by Governor Stevens, published in pamphlet.

The War Between the States, by A. H. Stephens.

War Records, vol. v., for Army of the Potomac in 1861; vol. vi., for Port Royal Expedition; vol. xiv., for James Island campaign; vol. xii., in three parts, for Pope's Campaign.

History of the 79th Highlanders, by William Todd.

History of the 21st Massachusetts, by General Charles F. Wolcott.

Biographical Register of West Point Graduates, by General George W. Cullum.

Defense of Charleston Harbor, by Major John Johnson.

Southern Historical Society Papers, vol. xvi.

Official dispatches of Admiral Dupont.

Life of Charles Henry Davis, Rear Admiral.

Letters and statements from gentlemen named in the Preface.

The author, having sought his information from original sources as far as possible, deems it unnecessary to mention the great number of histories, and biographies that he perused, as they throw little light on the subject, and much of that misleading.[379]

---

[379]Hazard Stevens' note. Hazard Stevens, *Life of Isaac Stevens,* vii-viii.

BIBLIOGRAPHY

A. Primary Sources

Public Documents

[Notes of the treaty proceedings of the Treaty of Mukilteo or Point Elliott], Treaty of
Mukilteo or Point Elliott, Treaty Papers 1854 & 1855, p 9 & 11, Microfilm Frame
No. 285 & 287 (Documents Relating to the Negotiations of Ratified and Unratified Treaties with Various Indian Tribes, 1801-69. T-494. 10 rolls), (National Archives Microfilm Publications T-494, roll 5), Records of the Bureau of Indian Affairs Record Group; 75, National Archives, Washington, D.C.

U.S. Department of Interior. Bureau of Indian Affairs. *Indian Tribes West of the Cascades*, by Isaac I. Stevens. Open-file report, Annual Report of the Office of Indian Affairs, 453. Washington, D.C., 1854.

Reminiscences

Graff, Ione Smith. "Memoirs of Dr. Henry A. Smith," 1957. The Seattle Museum of History and Industry, Seattle, Washington.

Kinnear, George, *Anti-Chinese Riots At Seattle, Wn., February 8th, 1886,* Seattle, Washington: Twenty-fifth Anniversary of Riots, February 8th, 1911, 17.

Meeker, Ezra, *Pioneer Reminiscences of the Puget Sound*; Library of American Civilization, LAC 13265. Chicago: Library Resources, 1970. Microfiche.

Oral History Project, Suquamish Tribal Archives, Suquamish Museum, Suquamish Washington.

Swan, James G. *The Northwest Coast or, Three Years' Residence in Washington Territory*. New York: Harper & Row Publishers, 1857; reprint, New York: J. & J. Harper Editions, 1969.

Letters

Arrowsmith, Jean, Lincoln, Vermont, to D. Ann Carver, Seattle, 29 April 1974. The Museum of History and Industry, Seattle, Washington.

Arrowsmith, William. Lincoln, Vermont, to Ms. Pryor, 30 July 1974, Washington Room, Washington State Capitol Library, Olympia, Washington.
_____. Bristol, Vermont, to Janice Krenmayr, Seattle, 6 January 1975. The Museum of History and Industry, Seattle, Washington.
_____. Baltimore, to Mary-Thadia D'Hondt, Seattle, 17 July 1980. The Museum of History and Industry, Seattle, Washington.
_____. Boston, Massachusetts, to Daniel Miller, Aptos, California, 26 November 1989, Daniel Miller, Aptos California.

Broderick, John C. Washington D.C., to Lennart Norl`en, Me`rida, Venezuela, 1 April 1977. Museum of History and Industry, Seattle, Washington

Claude, C. Cox. Fort Worth, Texas, to Rick Caldwell, Seattle, 20 August 1984. The Museum of History and Industry, Seattle, Washington.

Crawford, Richard C. Washington D.C., to Jodi Perlman-Cohen, Littleton, Colorado, 17 August 1976. The Museum of History and Industry, Seattle, Washington.
_____. to E. Nolan, Seattle, 2 November 1976. The Museum of History and Industry, Seattle, Washington.

Holm, Bill, Seattle, to Janice Krenmayr, Seattle, 10 January 1975. The Seattle Museum of History and Industry, Seattle, Washington.

Maxwell, Richard S., Washington, D.C., to Janice Krenmayr, Seattle, 18 September 1974. The Seattle Museum of History and Industry, Seattle, Washington.

Perry, Ted, Middlebury, Vermont, to Eli Gifford, Sebastopol, California, 15 October 1991. Eli Gifford, Sebastopol, California and The Museum of History and Industry, Seattle, Washington.
_____. to author, 25 October 1991. Eli Gifford, Sebastopol, California.
_____. to Michael Cook 30 October 1992. Eli Gifford, Sebastopol, California.
_____. *Home*, ed. John Stevens Dallas, Texas: Southern Baptist Radio and Television Commission, 1971.
_____. to author, 30 March 1997. Eli Gifford, Sebastopol, California

Rich, John M., Seattle, Washington, to Clarence B. Bagley, Seattle, Washington, "1930?",Transcription in the hand of John M. Rich, Clarence Bagley Papers, Manuscripts & University Archives Division, University of Washington, Seattle Washington.
_____. to Clarence B. Bagley, Seattle, Washington, replying to Bagley's letter of September 27, Transcription in the hand of John M. Rich, Clarence Bagley Papers, Manuscripts & University Archives Division, University of Washington, Seattle Washington.
_____. to Clarence B. Bagley, Seattle, Washington, "Dec. 7 1931", Transcription in the hand of John M. Rich, Clarence Bagley Papers, Manuscripts & University Archives Division, University of Washington, Seattle Washington.

Stevens, John, Fort Worth, Texas, to author, 17 March 1997. Eli Gifford, Sebastopol, California.

Wahrhaftig, Albert, Sebastopol, California to Daniel Markwyn, Rohnert Park, California, 1 April, 1997. wahrhaft@metro.net To daniel.markwyn@SONOMA.EDU.

Watt, Roberta Frye, Seattle, Washington, to Clarence B. Bagley, Seattle, Washington, 3 September 1931, Transcript in the hand of Roberta Frye Watt, Clarence Bagley Collection, Manuscripts & University Archives Division, University of Washington, Seattle, Washington.

_____. to Clarence B. Bagley, Seattle, Washington, 21 September1931, Transcript in the hand of Roberta Frye Watt, Clarence Bagley Collection, Manuscripts & University Archives Division, University of Washington, Seattle, Washington.

Interviews

Arrowsmith, William. Interview by author, 29 October 1991. Telephone.
_____. Interview by author, 1 December 1991. Telephone.
_____. Interview by author, 18 December 1991. Telephone.
_____. Interview by author, 18 February 1992. Telephone.

Buerge, David. Interview by author, 9 February 1993. Telephone.
_____. Interview by author, 12 March 1995. Telephone.

Caldwell, Rick. Interview by author 18 December1991. Telephone.

Jones, Marilyn. Interview by author, 12 November 1992. Telephone.
_____. Interview by author, 14 September 2007. Telephone.

Levesque, Ellen. Interview by author, 1992 11 November. Telephone.
_____. Interview by author, 4 February 1993. Telephone.

Stevens, John. Interview by the author, 30 April 1995, Sebastopol, California, Telephone.

Strauss, Stephen. Interview by the author, 3 July 1992, Sebastopol, California, Telephone.

Strong, Marilyn. Interview by the author, 11 November 1992. Sebastopol, California, Telephone.
_____. Interview by author, 7 February 1993, Sebastopol, California, Telephone.

183

B. Secondary Sources

Books

Avery, Mary W. *History and Government of the State of Washington.* Seattle: University of Washington Press, 1961, ix+583.

Bagley, Clarence B. *History of Seattle: A Volume of Memoirs and Genealogy of Representative Citizen of the City of Seattle and County of King Washington Including Biographies of Many of Those Who Have Past Away.* New York: Lewis Publishing Co., 1903.
_____. *History of King County Washington.* Vol. 1, Chicago, Seattle: The S. J. Clarke Publishing Co., 1929, 889.
_____. *History of Seattle: From the Earliest Settlements to the Present Time.* Vol. 1, Chicago: S.J. Clarke Publishing Co., 1916.

Brewster, David and David Buerge. *Washingtonians: Biographical Portrait of the State.* Seattle: Sasquatch Books, 1988.

Campbell, Joseph. *Power of Myth.* Interview by Bill Moyers, ed. Betty Sue Flowers. New York: Doubleday, 1988.

Cantwell, Robert. *The Hidden Northwest.* New York: J.B. Lippinnott Co., 1972, 335.

Costello, J. A. The Siwash Their Life Legends and Tales: Puget Sound and Pacific Northwest. Seattle: Calvert Co., 1895.

Daniels, Roger, ed., *Anti-Chinese Violence in North America.* New York: Arno Press, 1978, 103.

Dockstader, Frederick J. *Great North American Indians Profiles in Life and Leadership.* San Francisco: Van Nostrand Reinhold Co., 1977.

Dryden, Cecil. *Dryden's History of Washington.* Portland Oregon: 1968, 412.

Elmendorf, William W. *Twana Narratives: Native Historical Accounts of a Coast Salish Culture*. Seattle: University of Washington Press, 1993, iv+306.

Fairchild, Hoxie Neale. *The Noble Savage: A Study in Romantic Naturalism*. 2d ed. New York: Russell & Russell, 1928, xi+535.

Fischer, Robin. *Contact and Conflict: Indian-European Relations in British Columbia, 1774-1890*. Vancouver: University of British Columbia, 1977, xvi+250.

Galbraith, John S. *The Hudson's Bay Company As an Imperial Factor 1821 1869*. Berkeley: University of California Press, 1957, viii+ 500.

Gibbs, George. *Dictionary of the Chinook Jargon or Trade Language of Oregon*. New York: Cramoisy Press, 1865; reprint, New York: AMS Press Inc., 1970.

Gifford, Eli, and R. Michael Cook, eds. *How Can One Sell the Air*. Summertown, Tennessee: Book Publishing Co., 1992, reprint 2005.

Glassley, Ray Hoard. *Indian Wars of the Pacific Northwest*. By the author, City unknown, 1953; reprint, Portland: Binfords & Mort, 1972, xi+258.

Grant, Frederic James. *History of Seattle*. New York: American Publishing Co., 1891.

Hawthorn, H. B., C. S. Belshaw, and S. M. Damieson. *The Indian of British Columbia: A Study of Contemporary Social Adjustment*. Toronto: University of Toronto, 1960, ix+499.

Hunt, Herbert, and Floyd C. Kaylor. *Washington, West of the Cascades: Historical and Description: The Indian, Pioneer, The Modern*. Chicago: S. J. Clarke Co., 1917.

Jeffers, Susan. *Brother Eagle, Sister Sky*. New York: Dial Publisher, 1991.

Jones, L. T. *Aboriginal American Oratory*. Los Angeles: Southwest Museum, 1964.

Kaiser, Rudolf. "Chief Seattle's Speech(es): American Origins and European Reception," eds. Brian Swann and Arnold Krupat, *Recovering the Word*. Berkeley: Univ. Calif. Press, 1987, 497-536.

Marion, Cesare. "History of Western Washington Since 1846." In *Handbook of North American Indians Vol. 7 Northwest Coast*. ed. William Sturtevant, 169-79. Washington: Smithsonian Institute 1990, xv+777.

Martin, Calvin. *Keeper of the Game: Indian-Animal Relationships and the Fur Trade*. Berkeley: University of Ca. Press, 1978.

Meinig, D.W. *The Great Columbia Plain: A Historical Geography, 1805 1910*. Seattle: University of Washington Press, 1968, xxi+576.

Miller, Jay. *Shamanic Odyssey: The Lushoosteed Salish Journey to the Land of the Dead*. Menlo Park, California: Ballena Press, 1988, xviii+215.
_____. *Mourning Dove: A Salishan Autobiography*. Lincoln: University of Nebraska Press, 1990, xxxix+265.

Morgan, Murray. *Skid Row: An Informal Portrait of Seattle*. New York: Ballentine Books, 1960, 274.

Nesbit, Robert C. *He Built Seattle: A Biography of Judge Thomas Burke*. Seattle: University of Washington Press, 1961, xvii+455.

Richards, Kent D. *Isaac I. Stevens: Young Man in A Hurry*. Provo, Utah: Brigham Young University Press, 1979, xiv+484.

Rich, John M. *Seattle's Unanswered Challenge*. Seattle(?): privately printed, 1932. 2d ed. Fairfield, Washington: Ye Galleon Press, 1970.

Schwantes, Carlos A. *The Pacific Northwest: An Interpretive History*. Lincoln: University of Nebraska Press, 1989, xix+427.

Stevens, Hazard. *The Life of Isaac Ingalls Stevens*. Vol. 1 & 2. New York: Houghton, Mifflin and Co., 1901, xix+479.

Sturtevant, William, ed. *Handbook of North American Indians Vol. 7 Northwest Coast.* Washington: Smithsonian Institute 1990, xv+ 777.

Suttles, Wayne. *Coast Salish Essays.* Seattle: University of Washington Press, 1987, xiv+320.

Thomas, Edward Harper. *Chinook: A History of the Northwest Coast Trade Jargon,* Portland: Metropolitan Press, Publishers, 1935.

Thomas, Keith. *Man and the Natural World: A History of the Modern Sensibility.* New York: Pantheon Books, 426.

Tyler, Robert L. *Rebels of the Woods: the I.W.W. in the Pacific Northwest.* Eugene, Oregon: University of Oregon Books, 1967.

Vanderwerth, W. C., ed. *Indian Oratory.* With a Foreword by William R. Carmack. Norman: University of Oklahoma Press, 1971.

Vansina, Jan. *A Study in Historical Methodology.* trans. H. M. Wright, Chicago: Aldine Publishing Co., 1961, xvi+258.
_____. *Oral Tradition As History.* Madison, Wisconsin: University of Wisconsin Press, 1985, xiv+226

Wall, Steve, and Harvey Arden. *Wisdomkeepers: Meetings With Native Americans Spiritual Elders.* Hillsboro, Oregon: Beyond Words Publishing Co., 1990, 128.

Walens, Stanley. *Feasting with Cannibals: An Essay on Kwakiutl Cosmology.* Princeton, New Jersey: Princeton University Press, 1981, xi+192.

Warren, Sidney. *Farthest Frontier: The Pacific Northwest.* London: Kennikat, 1949, ix+375.

Watt, Roberta Frye. *The Story of Seattle.* Portland: Binford & Mort, 1932.

White, Lynn Jr. *Frontiers of Knowledge In the Study of Man.* New York: Harper & Brothers, 1956, xii+330.

_____. *Machina Ex Deo: Essays in the Dynamism of Western Culture*. Cambridge, Massachusetts: The MIT Press, 1968, ix+186.

Winther, Oscar Osburn. *The Great Northwest: A History*. 2d ed., New York: Alfred A. Knopf, 1960, xxx+491.

Wynne, David. *Reaction to the Chinese in the Pacific Northwest and British Columbia 1850 to 1910*. New York: Arno Press, New York Times Co., 1978, vi+511.

Zinn, Howard. *A People's History of the United States*. New York: Harper & Row, 1980.

Electronic Sources

"*Brother Eagle, Sister Sky* Review" Amazon.com: Books. n.d. Web. 24 Nov 2015.

Periodicals & Journals

Bagley, Clarence B. "Chief Seattle and Angeline." *Washington Historical Quarterly*. 22 (1931): 243-275.

The Catholic North West Progress, Vol. 67, No. 51, 18 December 1964, 9.

Carlson, Frank. *Chief Sealth*. Thesis, University of Washington, June 1903; reprint, Bulletin Series III No. 2, December, 1903, Seattle: University of Washington.

Churchill, Warren. "A Little Matter of Genocide: Native American Spirtuality and New Age Hucksterism" *Bloomsbury Review*, September/October 1988.

Clark, Jerry. "Thus Spoke Chief Seattle: The story of an Undocumented Speech" *Journal of the National Archives* Vol. 17 No. 1 (Spring 1985): 58-65.

Jaimes, M. Annette. "On *'Mother Earth'* An Interview with Russell Means," *Bloomsbury Review*, September/October 1988.

"The Decidedly Unforked Message of Chief Seattle." *Passages.*, Northwest Airlines Magazine, April 1974, 19-20.

"This earth is sacred," *Environmental Action,* 11 November 1972, 7.

"This earth is sacred" *Exclusively Yours,* April 1974, 31.

"For your children," *Wildlife Omnibus,* 15 November 1973, 30.

Karlin, Jules Alexander. "The Anti-Chinese Outbreaks in Seattle, 1885 1886" reprint, *The Pacific Northwest Quarterly,* Vol. 39, No. 2, Seattle, Washington, April, 1948.

Krenmayr, Janice. "'The earth is our mother.' Who really said that?" *The Seattle Times Sunday Magazine.* 5 January1975. 4-6.

"A Letter From Chief Seattle," *Outdoor America,* December 1975, 6.

Murray, Mary. "The Little Green Lie," *Reader's Digest,* July 1993, 100 104.

1996 Christmas Catalog. The Southwest Indian Foundation. Gallup, New Mexico.

Sapir, Edward. "The Social Organization of the West Coast Tribes" from the Transaction of the Royal Society of Canada Series III 1915 Vol. IX, Ottawa: Printed for the Royal Society of Canada 1915. Presented by Dr. Adam Shorff (Read) May Meeting 1915.

Newspapers

Buerge, David. "The Man We Call Seattle," *The Weekly,* 29 June – 5 July 1983, 24-27.
_____. "Isaac the Terrible: A Portrait of an Extraordinary Pioneer and Brilliant Explorer, Heroic Adventurer and Reckless Ruler," *Weekly: Seattle's News Magazine,* 28 August, 1985.
_____. "Seattle's King Arthur: How Chief Seattle continues to inspire his many admirers to put words in his mouth," *The Seattle Weekly* 17 July 1991, 27-29.

_____. "The Man Who Invented Chief Seattle", *Seattle Weekly*, 1 September 1993, 18-24.

Conover, C. T. "A Forgotten Pioneer Home, "*Seattle Sunday Times*, 22
	August 1948, 4.
_____. "Just Cogitating: Dr. Henry A. Smith Tells of Early Sound
	Life," *Seattle Sunday Times*, 17 August 1958, 6.
_____. "Just Cogitating: More Details Told of Dr. Henry Smith's Life,"
	The Seattle Times, Sunday 18 November 1956, 6.

Coombs, S. F. "Good Chief Seattle: How a Young Warrior Became
	Ruler of Many Tribes." *Post-Intelligencer*, 26 March 1893, 1.

Daily Post-Intelligencer, 12 July 1886, 2.

Krenmayr, Janice. "The earth is our mother.' Who really said that?" *The
	Seattle Times Sunday Magazine.* 5 January 1975, 4-6.

McDonald, Lucile. "Pioneer Doctor With Advanced Ideas." *Seattle
	Sunday Times Magazine*, 21 January 1960, 3.
_____. "Was Tslalakom Real Name of Chief Sealth?", *The Seattle Sunday
	Times*, 2 August 1964, 6.

Olympia, Washington Territory, 12 September 1856.

The Pioneer, Olympia, Washington, 11 January 1854, 1.
_____. *Pioneer and Democrat*, 26 October 1855, 1.
_____. *Pioneer and Democrat*, 21 December 1855, 2.
_____. *Pioneer and Democrat* , 10 April 1857, 1.

Post-Intelligencer, 29 October 1885, 1.
_____. *Post-Intelligencer*, 12 July 1886, 1.
_____. *Post Intelligencer*, 13 July 1886, 1.
_____. *Post-Intelligencer*, 26 March 1893, 1.

Seattle Daily Times, 15 April; 1, 5 May 1905.

Seattle Weekly, 3 September 1864, 1

Smith, Henry A. "Early Reminiscences Number Ten, Scraps From A
	Diary." *Seattle Sunday Star*, 29 October 1887, 7.
_____. *Weekly-Intelligencer*, 27 March 1871, 2.
_____. *Weekly-Intelligencer* 30 August 1873, 1.

Strauss, Stephen. "Mind and Matter," *The Globe and Mail*, 8 February 1992, 8 (D).

Suffia, David. "An early era of ill-feeling," *Seattle Time*, 12 March 1973, 13 (A).

Tarzan, Delores. "A Tribal Tribute." *The Seattle Times*, 14 September 1983, 1 (B).

Washington Republican , 5 June 1857, 2.

Weekly Intelligencer (Seattle), 25 April 1870, 1.

Unpublished Manuscripts

Bagley, Clarence. *Bagley's Scrapbook*, No. 5. Special Collections, Washington State University, Seattle, Washington.
_____. Clarence Bagley Papers, Manuscripts & University Archives Division, University of
Washington, Seattle Washington.

Miller, Daniel J. and Patricia R. "Chief Seattle's Speeches: An Example of History in the Making." "n.p." Photocopied.

Verwilgen, A. Felix. "Chief Sealth In the Letters of the First Christian Missionaries of the Puget Sound Area," paper presented at the Pioneer Association of the State of Washington by James Vernon Metcalfe, historian Pioneer Association of the State of Washington, May 1964, 12. The Museum of History and Industry, Seattle, Washington.

Made in the USA
Monee, IL
16 September 2021

78218156R00115